The Last Days CALENDAR

Understanding God's Appointed Times

THE Last Days CALENDAR

Understanding God's Appointed Times

Steven L. Sherman

Pleasant Word
A Division of WINEPRESS PUBLISHING

Printed in the United States of America

Packaged by Pleasant Word, a division of WinePress Publishing, PO Box 428, Enumclaw, WA 98022. The views expressed or implied in this work do not necessarily reflect those of Pleasant Word, a division of WinePress Publishing. Ultimate design, content, and editorial accuracy of this work are the responsibilities of the author.

Unless otherwise noted, all Scriptures are taken from the Holy Bible, New International Version, Copyright © 1973, 1978, 1984 by the International Bible Society. Used by permission of Zondervan Publishing House. The "NIV" and "New International Version" trademarks are registered in the United States Patent and Trademark Office by International Bible Society.

Scripture references marked KJV are taken from the King James Version of the Bible.

Scripture references marked NASB are taken from the New American Standard Bible, © 1960, 1963, 1968, 1971, 1972, 1973, 1975, 1977 by The Lockman Foundation. Used by permission.

ISBN 1-57921-587-4
Library of Congress Catalog Card Number: 2003100417

Will there really be a "secret rapture?"
When might the rapture take place?
How is Antichrist to be revealed?

A new understanding of the chronology and nature of end time events as revealed through the Hebrew calendar and the festivals of the Lord.

Table of Contents

Foreword

Purpose and Intent

Numerous books, magazine articles, and tracts have concerned eschatology (the biblical study of last things) in recent years. Some of these written works were intended for a general audience. Other texts and essays, composed by theologians, are strictly for other scholars' review. Much of the theological terminology found in the latter group is foreign to the average reader.

The common person has scant knowledge of biblical terms and events. Others, who attend church on a regular basis, have not read the Bible in its entirety or have read it without delving thoroughly into its prophecy treasures. My first purpose in writing *The Last Days Calendar* was to reach both categories of readers—enlightening people with little or no Bible knowledge and bringing new insight concerning end time events to more seasoned Bible students.

To accomplish this first purpose, definitions or explanations of biblical and theological terms frequently appear following words or expressions the first time they appear in the text. Since the Word of God is divinely inspired and the ultimate source and standard of truth, full Scripture quotations and references immediately follow verses or passages cited to afford the reader an opportunity to fact check or challenge my statements.

I invite the reader to act as did the believers in Berea, who "were of more noble character than the Thessalonians, for they received the message with great eagerness and examined the Scriptures every day" (Acts 17:11). Please review the concepts presented in this book to line them up with your understanding or to find them disproved in God's Word. I welcome all correspondence, positive or negative in review, on the concepts presented herein. The scope of prophetic Scripture as it unfolds in the coming future holds such awesome terrors for the unbeliever and challenges for the Bible believer that anyone with compassion for others' suffering would welcome refutation of basic tribulation concepts, right?

A second intention in writing this book was to explain and help interpret biblical prophecies (100% accurate predictions of future events), looking at many through the context of the Hebraic and Hellenic cultures in which God's spokespersons delivered their messages. Light may be shed through knowledge regarding contemporary customs as prophecies were first received. As a Jewish believer in Christ, a natural-born descendant of Jacob and the Jewish people, I utilize background knowledge to help the reader understand both Old and New Testament passages and hopefully help interpret prophetic messages for our modern audience.

Now one vital key, *the* key to understanding Bible prophecy in context, is the fact that all Old Testament Scripture (the Hebrew Scriptures, or *Tanakh*) proclaim Jesus Christ as the true Messiah sent to redeem the world.

Just as the first coming of Jesus Christ to Earth was promised in numerous places in the Old Testament, there are clear passages and symbolic pictures and allusions to the Second Coming of Christ. An understanding of the feasts, fasts, and festivals found in the Old Testament, for example, with their frequent descriptions of the nature of Jesus Christ in His person, is therefore most valuable in comprehending Bible prophecy. For one example, God Himself used the traditional Jewish wedding ceremony as illustration of His relationship to the Church, the body of true Christian believers. Therefore, knowledge of Jewish betrothal and marriage customs can be most helpful to interpret the meaning of Christ's wedding illustration(s) in its proper context (see chapter 18). For another example, knowledge of customs associated with synagogue services of Bible times could heighten our understanding of Jesus' teaching in His role as the finest Jewish rabbi (teacher) ever.

The third purpose motivating the writing of this book was to present my viewpoint, which developed and emerged over several years of intense study, challenging certain prevalent interpretations of Bible prophecies regarding the last days of Earth. Points in question include tribulation theories and misunderstandings concerning believers' endurance, "date setting" Christ's return, a "secret" rapture, etc.

I have striven for the highest possible accuracy in sharing the concepts presented within and have sought to share my heart with you, the reader, in a concise manner and in simple terms. May the Lord Himself richly bless the reading of this book and consume any controversy it stirs in minds sincerely fixed on plumbing the truths of the Bible, to His own glory.

Steven L. Sherman

Preface and Acknowledgments

"I had not intended to write a book on prophecy . . ."

I had not intended to write a book on prophecy. These pages stem from a wonderfully rich home Bible study. After ten years of personally searching the Scriptures and having taught through several books of the Bible, I was afforded the privilege of teaching through the Book of Revelation at my church. Due to the numbers in attendance, it was necessary to adhere to a lecture format, utilizing a microphone. When that series was over, several friends desired to study prophecy further in an intimate atmosphere.

Sometime after we started, the new weekly Bible study group received from me what amounts to one chapter of this book at each of our meetings. The saints were delighted to learn prophecy in this manner and were always encouraging with an expectant "What excitement comes next week?" attitude. I gratefully acknowledge their help in poring over the text of this work, correcting and clarifying where necessary, and for their faithfulness and prayer support.

For me, the writing of this book was not a burden but a delight. The real work that took place was in its editing. The Bible study was originally typed and the data had to be input into a computer. In addition, the material needed to be edited, bullet points made, fonts for titles selected, chapter summaries created, and so much more. I thank my precious Lord and Savior for Matt Sherman. Matt is my first-born son and my brother in Christ. I can never repay him for the countless hours he sacrificed working to get this book in a presentable format.

A special acknowledgment of gratitude is extended to a wonderful Christian brother and a successful professional athlete—Anthony Pleasant. Because of his personal encouragement and faithfulness, in both prayer and financial support of my ministry, this book was able to be published.

This prophetic literary work is based upon the inerrant, divinely inspired Word. It was birthed of a group of committed Christians who desired to grow in the grace and knowledge of Jesus Christ. May it bless all of those who read it and glorify our heavenly Father.

Steven Sherman

Introduction for Students of the Bible

First of all, you must understand that in the last days scoffers will come, scoffing and following their own evil desires. They will say, "Where is this 'coming' he promised?"

—2 Peter 3:3–4a

In our foreseeable future even those who have enjoyed expression of religious freedoms will be persecuted for faith in Christ. As they are dragged to prison and even martyrdom, will they will be ridiculed with "Where is this coming your Jesus promised?"

Millions of American Christians anticipate a secret and silent pre-tribulation rapture, whisking them away to the glorious marriage supper of the Lamb. This concept is alluring. Massive book and video sales centering on the rapture theme are today's best sellers. Many strong evangelical movements hold to this doctrine in their statements of faith; many Christian educators do not present the pre-tribulation rapture as one of several theories or possible interpretations but as fact.

It *would* be a source of comfort to not pass through a coming great tribulation. Although this doctrine has wide appeal, does existing biblical evidence confirm it as truth?

It is helpful in understanding eschatology that the book of Revelation is considered as first and foremost an epistle addressed to Christ's Church. Although the Apocalypse represents mixed genres, its symbols, when properly interpreted, help encourage and exhort Christian believers. Revelation's prophecies were declared a millennia ago for the benefit of God's Church as much as for the coming "tribulation saints." The foreknowledge of the end of the age has been revealed to the elect so that the elect will be encouraged to stand firm even while facing death. As psychologist and Holocaust survivor Victor Frankl put it, "The last of our human freedoms is to choose our attitude in any given circumstances." Understanding Revelation and other biblical end times prophecies grants us increased sagacity to make wise attitude choices in the face of martyrdom and death.

Indeed Christ shall return for His Church, but will its purity shine from the fires of tribulation persecution? My new work, developed from individual and group-led prophecy study over more than a decade, provides fresh insight concerning:

- the ministry of the "144,000"
- the "two witnesses"
- the nature, purposes, and populace of those who will dwell in the coming millennial kingdom
- the possible timing of the rapture, return of Christ, and fulfillments of biblical festivals
- many more prophetic insights

A Jewish believer, I have not only prepared this volume through intensive study of hundreds of Revelation-parallel biblical passages but have helped amplify the meaning and symbolism of Bet Hillelstyled synagogue liturgy and the traditions associated with the biblical Levitical festivals and other Jewish observances, a fascinating study for any Christian. I have brought the benefits of interpreting the Scriptures in the light of their original culture and context settings.

Jesus Christ fulfilled the spring cycle of biblical festivals in His First Advent by instituting the New Covenant at the Passover, being entombed during the Feast of Unleavened Bread, resurrecting on the Festival of Firstfruits and sending the promised Holy Spirit at Pentecost.

What does the Bible reveal concerning the Second Coming and the fulfillment of the wheat and grape harvests, the Feast of Trumpets, Day of Atonement, and the Jubilee?

I believe that I have been able to make a clear connection between the "fall cycle" of biblical festivals and the return of Christ as well as have shed new light on Chanukah (the Feast of Dedication of John 10), Talmudic statements regarding Messiah's coming(s), and much more. I also explore, in ways that are moving for the reader and simple to follow, clear passages of Scripture concerning the some of the many allusions and "types" found in the Old Testament and in Jewish tradition that help clarify apocalyptic passages.

····················

Chapter 1

After Distress . . .

"If those days had not been cut short, no one would survive, but for the sake of the elect those days will be shortened."

—Matthew 24:22

To better understand this prophetic verse concerning end time events, we need to examine the context in which Jesus Christ spoke it. Matthew 24 is part of a passage Bible theologians (people studying the knowledge of, nature of, and doctrines of God) have labeled, "The Olivet Discourse."

"No one would survive, but for the sake of the elect . . ." Jesus spoke these words while sitting on the Mount of Olives and communicating a discourse, a lengthy and formal answer to a several-faceted question from His disciples. According to the three Bible accounts of The Olivet Discourse (Matthew 24–25; Mark 13; Luke 21), Jesus had just left from speaking publicly to the crowds in front of the temple in Jerusalem. As He walked on, His disciples remarked how beautiful and massive the stones were that adorned the gorgeous temple buildings. Jesus replied that "the time will come when not one stone would be left on another; every one of them will be thrown down . . ." (Matthew 24:2); a prophetic event that history records occurred in A.D. 70.

Jesus had walked from the temple to the Mount of Olives. This mount is due east of Jerusalem and faces opposite the temple's entrance, which faced eastward to the mount. The mount rises today to a height of about 2,700 feet, some two hundred feet higher than the frequently mentioned Bible mount of Zion. Jesus and His disciples were afforded a magnificent view overlooking the city and especially the temple itself.

As Jesus was seated and perhaps looked toward the temple entrance, Peter, James, John, and Andrew came to ask Him a question privately: "Tell us," they said, "when will this happen, and what will be the sign of your coming and of the end of the age?" (Matthew 24:3b). Jesus offered a lengthy and detailed reply (Matthew 24:4–51) and after that the parable of the ten virgins, the parable of the talents, and His account of the sheep and the goats (Matthew 25).

Parables are illustrative and memorable stories designed to convey truth. The parables of Matthew 25, among others, are known as Kingdom Parables, prophecies of a future time when Jesus Christ as King Messiah will reign supremely on Earth. The term "Messiah" is from the Hebrew "*moshiach*," a term meaning "anointed," that when translated to the Greek is "*Christos*," our English "Christ." The Hope of Israel, the Messiah, would be the One on whom God would pour out His Spirit (Isaiah 11:2).

In Bible times, Hebrew kings and priests, and often, prophets, were anointed with oil, symbolizing an anointing outpouring of God's Holy Spirit. The Messiah would fulfill all three anointed offices in one person. He would be a magnificent Prophet (delivering God's word to His people), Priest (who intercedes on behalf of His people before God), and King (who rules His people with God-ordained authority).

Jesus replied in part to the questions of Matthew 24 concerning the end of the age with parables of the coming Messianic kingdom. The parable of the ten virgins looks at a bridegroom (Jesus Christ), a long time in "returning" (time between Christ's ascension to Heaven after His resurrection and His return to Earth for His Church) for his "bride."

> "At that time the kingdom of heaven will be like ten virgins who took their lamps and went out to meet the bridegroom. Five of them were foolish and five were wise. The foolish ones took their lamps but did not take any oil with them. The wise, however, took oil in jars along with their lamps. The bridegroom was a long time in coming, and they all became drowsy and fell asleep. At midnight the cry rang out: 'Here's the bridegroom! Come out to meet him!' Then all the virgins woke up and trimmed their lamps. The foolish ones said to the wise, 'Give us some of your oil; our lamps are going out.' 'No,' they replied, 'there may not be enough for both us and you. Instead, go to those who sell oil and buy some for yourselves.' But while they were on their way to buy the oil, the bridegroom arrived. The virgins who were ready went in with him to the wedding banquet. And the door was shut. Later the others also came. 'Sir! Sir!' they said. 'Open the door for us!' But he replied, 'I tell you the truth, I don't know you.' Therefore keep watch, because you do not know the day or the hour." Matthew 25:1–13

The biblical "virgin" may symbolize spiritual purity, specifically, one who is not guilty of idolatry. Biblically speaking, individuals or even nations guilty of idolatry or spiritual fornication are known as "adulterers" or "prostitutes." Israel is called a brazen prostitute and an adulterous wife in Ezekiel 16.

When the "cry rang" to meet the bridegroom in the parable of Matthew 24, foolish virgins were left unprepared, and their lamps were extinguished for lack of oil. Oil is a natural material that symbolizes the presence of the indwelling Holy Spirit in the believer. The Holy Spirit resides permanently inside the Christian believer.

The term "fool" in the parable means "unbeliever." For example, "a fool says to himself in his heart, 'God does not exist'" (see Psalm 14:1; 53:1). Before the bridegroom returns (the end of the age), each person going to Heaven must have oil in their lamp (become a true believer).

It is essential to note that in Christ's parable, once the door to the wedding feast was shut, no one further was allowed to enter. Those who attempted to fill their lamps following the return of the groom were left outside, ultimately, in "outer darkness" (one Bible description of eternal judgment in Hell). Today is the day of salvation, dear reader!

The "foolish virgins" may have looked like they were indeed pure. They may have been very religious persons. They may have heard of the groom's coming return for His bride. Similarly, there are today churchgoers who have read the Bible, heard sermons, served in church, and prayed regularly. These things cannot atone for sin. God has already paid a price for your "lamp oil." Jesus Christ purchased men for God with His atoning blood (Revelation 5:9). Through faith may God's gift of grace, eternal life, be received (Ephesians 2:8–9). The individual must trust in Jesus Christ for salvation or else, when He returns for His bride (the true, believing Church), the door will be shut and outsiders will be cast to damnation.

Note that the disciples' question in Matthew 24 actually has two parts to it:

As Jesus was sitting on the Mount of Olives, the disciples came to him privately. "Tell us," they said, "when will this [destruction of Herod's temple] happen, and what will be the sign of your [second] coming [to earth from heaven] and of the end of the [this present] age?" Matthew 24:3

They are asking a twofold question: 1) When is it that Herod's Temple will be destroyed? 2) What will be the sign of Your triumphant return at the end of this age?

The prophecy Jesus gave concerning the second temple in Jerusalem was specific and unique. Jesus not only predicted the temple's destruction but that every one of the massive stones would be removed so that "no stone remained on another." According to an ancient historian, Josephus, as chronicled in his *The Antiquities of the Jews*, some of the temple stones were as large as thirty-seven feet in length, a dozen feet high, and eighteen feet wide, each. This prophecy of destruction was fulfilled in A.D. 70 by General Titus' Roman army, who completely destroyed Jerusalem and its temple buildings, including the separating of all temple stones.

Titus had issued orders to preserve the temple and its furnishings as victory trophies to the Romans, when a stray torch tossed into the sanctuary resulted in a devastating fire. Gold ornamentation throughout and gold leaf on the temple roof melted from the intense heat, liquefied, and collected in the spaces between the temple stones. The stones needed to be pried apart, each from every other, after the fire ended and the base structure cooled so the greedy Romans could collect their melted gold. All that remains today from this wondrous structure is its foundation.

The second part of the disciples' question included a request to Jesus to identify a miraculous sign announcing the end of the age. A supernatural phenomenon was eagerly sought, just as the First Advent (the incarnation and birth of Christ) was preceded by a miraculous sign, the annunciation of a virgin birth:

"Therefore the Lord himself will give you a sign: The virgin will be with child and will give birth to a son, and will call him Immanuel." Isaiah 7:14

The sign of the coming of the Son of God was an "earthly" sign, a natural occurrence of birth, albeit a supernaturally-conceived child. Jesus, born of a virgin, was birthed in a stable and worshipped by humble shepherds. The sign of the Christ's Second Coming will be in stark contrast, a heavenly sign:

"At that time the sign of the Son of Man will appear in the sky, and all the nations of the earth will mourn. They will see the Son of Man coming on the clouds of the sky with power and great glory." Matthew 24:30

The very King of Kings, resurrected and glorified, will shine brighter than the noon day Sun and reign on Earth, but if "those days had not been cut short, no one would survive, but for the sake of the elect those days will be shortened." (See Matthew 24:22.)

The term "those days" refers to the period immediately preceding the heavenly sign announcing the glorious appearing of Christ. "Those days" at the end of the age are characterized by great distress:

"For then there will be great distress, unequaled from the beginning of the world until now—and never to be equaled again." Matthew 24:21

The elect (those who will inherit eternal life) are subject to tremendous persecution just before the return of Jesus Christ to Earth. Within this time of unparalleled suffering will come worldwide suffering from God's righteous judgment, so great in fact, that if this time was not "cut short" as Jesus said, the utter annihilation of man would be the end result.

"If those days had not been cut short, no one would survive, but for the sake of the elect those days will be shortened . . . immediately after the distress of those days . . . the sign of the Son of Man will appear in the sky . . ." Matthew 24:22–30

The saints of God will be rescued out of the great distress as the Lord sends angels with a loud trumpet call to gather them to Heaven, cutting short their persecution on the earth. The elect are those Christian believers meeting Christ in the air before His return to the earth to establish His kingdom on Earth. This event is commonly known as the "rapture" of the church. (See 1 Thessalonians 4:13–18.)

Let us examine the given Bible timeline carefully. [I realize that many rapture-believing scholars place the rapture at a different juncture, as will be addressed later in this book.] For the sake of the elect those days are "cut short." The elect will suffer great distress until the rapture. The rapture does not occur until the sign of the Son Man appears in the sky. The sign itself does not appear until after the distress of those days. In other words, placed in order of occurrence:

1. Distress of those days—days cut short for the sake of God's elect
2. Sign of the Son of Man
3. The rapture

Jesus Christ said of these difficult times, "All men will hate you because of me, but he who stands firm to the end will be saved" (Matt. 10:22).

A defense of the timing of the rapture as outlined here, plus much insight into the events surrounding the tribulation, rapture, and coming reign of Christ on Earth follows.

Summary of Chapter One

- Christ promised to end, coincident with His triumphant return to Earth, days of intense persecution for God's people.
- In the midst of Christ's return, the Bible also warns of cataclysmic suffering so great, life itself is in danger of being extinguished. Just when "those days" are "cut short" is of vital interest to anyone facing such difficulties on Earth.
- The Bible speaks of hardship and persecution of the true follower of Christ, but great is the reward in Heaven for those who are persecuted for righteousness sake. (See Matthew 5:10–12.)

Kept "from the Hour of Trial" . . . So How Long is an Hour, Anyway?

"Since you have kept my command to endure patiently, I will keep you from the hour of trial that is going to come upon the whole world to test those who live upon the earth."

—Revelation 3:10

There is a prevalent Bible doctrine (Bible teaching, Bible subject) taught today across America, which states that the Church will be raptured (captured out of, physically removed from, the earth) before *those days* of great distress foretold of by Jesus Christ during The Olivet Discourse. This doctrine is called by theologians the pre-tribulation (before the period of tribulation) view of the rapture.

Those who hold to this view of the timing of the rapture (that it occurs before "those days" commence) state that the rapture occurs immediately preceding the seven-year period of tribulation before the return of Jesus Christ.

So, what is the seven-year tribulation? In the Bible, in the book of Daniel, its ninth chapter, are prophetic passages concerning periods of time referred to as "sevens." "Seven" is the meaning of the Hebrew word used in Daniel chapter nine, "*shabua.*" This term for "seven" (translated less than literally as "week" in many English Bible versions) when found in Daniel is interpreted to connote a seven-year period of time. The reason that Bible scholars have determined that in Daniel "seven" means seven *years* (a "week" of years) is based in part upon the Bible law concerning the "Sabbath of Years."

The nation of Israel was commanded to observe the seventh day as a day of rest, or Sabbath (Exodus 20:8–11), and also to observe every seventh year as a year of "rest for the land" (the land lies fallow and "rests" from the taxing labors of agricultural production). This seventh year is known as the Sabbatical Year:

> "But in the seventh year the land is to have a Sabbath of rest, a Sabbath to the LORD. Do not sow your fields or prune your vineyards." Leviticus 25:4

Israel, as the Bible records, never observed this regulation. This act of disobedience and others, including intermarriage with neighboring idolatrous nations, idol worship, and sins of the Israelites, resulted in the Israelites being taken captive to Babylon.

Daniel wrote regarding the "sevens" during the time when many Jews were serving as captives in Babylon in the sixth century B.C. Daniel understood that according to God's Word, as revealed to the prophet Jeremiah, the desolation of Jerusalem would last seventy years (Daniel 9:2). Indeed, this captivity lasted for exactly seventy years to the day as was prophesied by Jeremiah (Jeremiah 25:12). Why seventy years' time of captivity? Each single year of captivity was punishment for every seven-year period the Sabbath Year regulation was ignored. For 490 years, the people of Israel had failed to observe the Sabbatical Year regulation, totaling seventy missed Sabbatical Year observances. Seventy years of captivity was the punishment for their failure.

As an aside: This special time of punishment was foretold long before Israel acted in disobedience. Leviticus 26:14–46 speaks of degrees of punishment to the people of Israel for disobedience. When Israel would refuse to carry out the commands of the Lord and violate His covenant, the Lord would bring disease and defeat to the nation, and much of the Old Testament narrative describes this process. The people would then be taken into captivity by their enemies:

> "then the land will enjoy its Sabbath years all the time that it lies desolate and you are in the country of your enemies; then the land will rest and enjoy its Sabbaths." Leviticus 26:34

Judah was taken to seventy years' captivity so the land possessed by the tribal clan of Judah and the city of Jerusalem were desolate for that time. The land had seventy consecutive years of Sabbath rests for the 490 years of disobedience, as outlined above.

When discussing the seventy years of captivity, it is essential to note that our modern day Julian calendar is based on the passage of time it takes our Earth to revolve once around our Sun—a "solar year" of 365 and one-quarter days' duration. In contrast, the Bible calendar was based on a 360–day "lunar year," twelve lunar months comprised of thirty days each. Our modern calendar requires a periodic leap year every four years to compensate for the quarter day ending each solar year. Likewise, the Hebrew calendar required a periodic additional month, a thirteenth month, to compensate for the five and one-quarter uncounted days on the 360–day calendar so festivals and observances would not shift through the seasons of the year. *All Bible dates must be interpreted in the light of the 360–day lunar calendar*, and the reader should be wary of prophecy interpretations expounding upon a Julian method.

Now a special "seven" was foretold to Daniel:

> "He will confirm a covenant with many for one 'seven.' In the middle of the 'seven' he will put an end to sacrifice and offering. And on a wing of the temple he will set up an abomination that causes desolation until the end that is decreed is poured out on him." Daniel 9:27

This passage of Scripture parallels a seven-year time outlined in the book of Revelation. One seven is a period of seven years or a "week of years." "In the middle of the seven" refers to the exact time halfway through the seven-year period—after three and one-half years—of great difficulty have elapsed.

In the book of Revelation there is a time period of forty-two months mentioned more than once. (See Revelation 11:2; 13:5.) Forty-two months equals three and one-half biblical, lunar calendar years. This special period of three and one-half years, which begins at the start of the seven-year tribulation period, is equivalent to Daniel's "middle of the seven" [years]. We again see three and one-half years represented in Revelation 11:3 and 12:6 as a 1,260–day period. Thirty days per lunar month multiplied by forty-two months equals 1,260 days. Certainly, 360 days in a lunar calendar year multiplied by three and one-half equals 1,260 days also. Therefore, the terms "middle of the seven," "three and one-half years," "forty-two months," and "1,260 days" as used throughout this book are equivalent terms.

The one who sets up an abomination (Antichrist's idol, or image, of himself) causing desolation (Jewish people, refusing to bow to an idol, fleeing Jerusalem) affirms a covenant (an accord, or pact) with the Jewish people for a "period of time," specifically, seven lunar, or biblical years. This charismatic leader depicted in the Bible, the Antichrist, violates the "agreement" halfway through the covenant, three and one-half years following its signing, and sets his image for worship as God. (See Revelation 13:15.) Following the erection of this image, the second half of Daniel's last "seven," one-half the seven-year period at the end of the age, is a time of great persecution and distress for the God's elect. (See Revelation 12:17; 13:7.)

Again, there are those who hold to the pre-tribulation interpretation of the rapture, stating that the Church is raptured at the beginning, not following the middle or near the end of, the seven-year tribulation period. Therefore, those jailed or martyred for their faith in Jesus Christ during this period are not part of the Church but are called "tribulation saints." (Since the Church was raptured at the beginning of the tribulation, new converts to the faith must have been made to become those believers in Christ who endure the great distress of "those days.") It should be noted that mighty people of God, great scholars and defenders of the faith, have studied the Scriptures carefully and fathomed a pre-tribulation rapture theory.

This theory is, in part, based on examining two key passages of Scripture regarding the tribulation: 1) "For God did not appoint us to suffer wrath but to receive salvation through our LORD Jesus Christ" (1 Thess. 5:9). All pre-millennial scholars (those who believe in a coming, literal thousand-year reign of Christ on Earth) whether they subscribe to a pre—, mid—(middle of the seven), post—, or pre-wrath rapture of the Church, agree that the Christian is raptured just before God's wrath is poured upon an unbelieving world. These divergent views of the rapture simply disagree as to when the wrath is consummated, an issue I will take up later in this work. 2) "Since you have kept my command to endure patiently, I will keep you from the hour of trial that is going to come upon the whole world to test those who live upon the earth" (Revelation 3:10).

Again, when does the wrath pour out? May a time frame be fixed for the hour of trial of Revelation 3:10? Note that the verse under discussion reads: "I will keep you from the *hour* of trial . . ." (emphasis mine). Revelation does not say, "I will keep you from the *seven-year period* of trial," nor has God written here "eighty-four months," "2,520 days" or any other seven-year statement in this verse. Rather, verse 10 speaks specifically of an *hour* of trial. Indulge me in a bit of speculation if you will.

1. Daniel's week is understood as seven "days"; each day represents one year's time, a lunar year of 360 days' length.
2. One *hour* is one twenty-fourth of one day (twenty-four hours in each lunar day). If Daniel's "day" equals one year, then one "hour" of prophetic Scripture, therefore, would be one twenty-fourth of 360 days or a period of fifteen days! (It is interesting to note that the earth's sphere of 360 degrees is divided into twenty-four time zones. The earth rotates fifteen degrees of longitude every hour.)
3. What if, therefore, the outpouring of God's final wrath was to occur over fifteen days rather than the whole seven years of Daniel's "seven?"
4. I will take up this issue later in this book, for my understanding is that the "*days cut short*" mentioned by Jesus Christ refers to a specific fifteen-day period *cut short* to a ten-day period for the outpouring of God's wrath on the world, a two-thirds chunk of "one hour." (Compare this notion of two-thirds or two of three with Hosea 6:2 and Zechariah 13:8, by the way.)
5. The elect (the universal Church comprised of all true believers) will be on Earth during a time of great persecution but will be removed (raptured) prior to the final outpouring of God's wrath on Earth.

At His First Advent, Jesus Christ made His triumphal entry into Jerusalem, riding "lowly upon a donkey's colt," on the tenth day of the first month of the Bible calendar, the month of Nisan. This tenth day of Nisan is also the biblical day when the Passover lamb is to be selected for sacrifice (as in Exodus 12:3). Today, millions worldwide also know this day as Palm Sunday (palm fronds were laid down at the feet of King Jesus).

Later in that month of Nisan, Jesus partook of the Last Supper with His disciples and instituted the "New Covenant in His blood" on the eve of the Passover. He was then crucified and entombed during the biblical Feast of Unleavened Bread. After, Jesus resurrected from the dead on the day when the Feast of First Fruits was to be celebrated. As part of the feast, a sheaf of the first grain harvested was given as a wave offering on the day after the Sabbath of the Passover week. (See Leviticus 23:9–14.) Jesus, who is also the "Firstfruits of the Resurrection" (see 1 Corinthians 15:23), rose from the dead on the day following the Sabbath (the Sabbath falls on the seventh day of each week).

The tomb of Jesus Christ was found empty early on Sunday morning (biblical first day of each week), following the "Passion Week" (really eight days, the seven-day week plus one day, counting from the triumphal entry to Christ's resurrection; Palm Sunday to Resurrection Sunday).

Fifty days later, at the end of the biblical Feast of Weeks, the Holy Spirit descended in power on the disciples of Christ on Pentecost. Truly the Law of Moses is fulfilled in Christ! (See Luke 24:44; Colossians 2:17.)

The point: These first four major biblical festivals/feasts of Leviticus 23 (Passover, Unleavened Bread, Firstfruits, and Weeks) were fulfilled in both their happenstance and in the person of Christ ("natural" and "spiritual" fulfillment) at the First Advent, or first coming, of Christ to Earth. We can rest assured that the last three of the seven major Bible festivals will also have their natural and spiritual fulfillment in the person of Christ at His Second Coming, the subject of much of this book and one Bible key to understanding the literal return of Jesus Christ as conquering King.

So, what three events of Leviticus 23 await Christ's return to be fulfilled? The last three festivals, or fall cycle, of biblical festivals are: Rosh HaShona (Feast of Trumpets); Yom Kippur (Day of Atonement); and Sukkot (Feast of Tabernacles), which take place during the first fifteen days of the seventh month (Tishri), on the Bible/Jewish calendar. These festivals that the Lord established are all intense pictures of Christ. The time span of fifteen days (two weeks and one day) in which the last three festivals are to be celebrated, I believe, relate significantly to the fifteen-day period, or biblical "hour," of God's wrath upon those who live on the earth (Revelation 3:10).

Biblical Christians will be kept away from the "hour" of God's wrath but will endure through much of the distress of "those (1,260) days." Thankfully (or no flesh would be saved), those 1,260 days will be cut short, that is, abbreviated, so that no one will be able to calculate Christ's return for Christians at the rapture, but they will long and pine for it.

> "But for the sake of the elect those days will be shortened." Matthew 24:22b

In the next chapter we will seek to gain insight into the meaning of the "pouring out of God's wrath" to determine what exactly it is and how it might occur!

Summary of Chapter Two

- I agree with many biblical scholars that true followers of Christ will be kept from the "hour of trial" spoken of in Revelation 3:10.

- I propose that the "hour" referred to in Revelation refers to a fifteen-day period of time, cut short to ten days of intense trials for the surviving remnant of God's chosen people.
- Four great events of Scripture, encapsulated in Leviticus 23, were literally fulfilled at Christ's First Advent. The other three await fulfillment at His return and occur on the Bible calendar in a ten-day period.
- I am presenting these concepts in part to refute the popular pre-tribulation theory (which states that Jesus Christ will come at the beginning of the seven years of tribulation at the rapture for the saints) based upon the biblical definition of time periods presented herein. In contrast, a different timeline of the events of the tribulation will be presented.

Chapter 3

The "Completion"
of God's Wrath

To properly interpret prophetic passages relating to the "confirmation of the covenant" spoken of in the book of Daniel, we must make a distinction between the general term, "God's wrath," and the specific biblical "completion of" or "outpouring of" God's wrath.

In John's gospel we receive excellent insight into the term "God's wrath":

> "Whoever believes in the Son has eternal life, but whoever rejects the Son will not see life, for God's wrath remains on him."
> John 3:36

John declares under inspiration that *God's wrath* remains upon (was on in past and will continue upon in future) each person who, unto death, rejects Jesus Christ as Savior. This person will "not see life." Since each living person is today physically alive, the rejection of Jesus Christ that John writes of relates to the spiritual, inward life. Any person who rejects Christ's atonement and resurrection from the dead is rejecting God's sole provision for human salvation—payment for sin through the substitutionary sacrifice of God's Son on the cross.

To better understand the biblical concepts of God's wrath and one's spiritual life, we must examine Scriptures relating to sin (literally, missing the mark of perfection or coming short of God's holy perfection) and judgment. God's wrath remains on those who remain in a state of sin—because they reject Christ.

For all have sinned and fall short of the glory of God. Romans 3:23

Surely I was sinful at birth, sinful from the time my mother conceived me. Psalm 51:5

We are spiritually separated from God from the moment of conception. Though God's providence and benevolence are upon those tender youths whom God views as "moral innocents," this state of separation is eternal for those more adult individuals who reject Christ. Those who reject Christ spend eternity separated from God in Hell:

For the wages of sin is [eternal] death . . . Romans 6:23a

At birth, we emerge physically alive from the womb but spiritually dead inside. We are conceived in sin (we are children of Adam and Eve through fornication) and are born spiritually dead. This Bible doctrine is different than the heinous concept of "original sin" proposed by St. Augustine, which states the sin nature of infants and young children condemns them to eternal punishment should they die in their youth!

[Author's note: Original sin is often used as an anti-Christian talking point by Muslim or Jewish apologists who recognize how God's sovereignty and mercy might apply in dealing with those unable to comprehend atonement such as small children and those with mental disabilities! St. Augustine was misinterpreting Romans 5, which clearly states that "not only has death passed from Adam to man" but that "all men have sinned themselves and stand judged as individuals apart from Adam's transgression," as in Romans 5:12.]

> "Surely the arm of the LORD is not too short to save, nor His ear too dull to hear. But your iniquities have separated you from your God; your sins have hidden His face from you so that he will not hear." Isaiah 59:1–2

We have all sinned. Sinners, apart from Christ, face sin's ultimate penalty—death. God's wrath remains on sinners who reject Jesus Christ. Separated from God for eternity, God's wrath remains on them, and they experience condemnation to Hell, the "second death."

> He who has the Son has life; he who does not have the Son of God does not have life. 1 John 5:12

The good news is that the spiritually dead sinner, separated from God, can be made spiritually alive, reconciled to God, and come under the blessings of God through saving faith in Jesus Christ! One way Jesus defined this new spiritual life was by the term "born again."

In John 3:1–21, a man named Nicodemus visits Jesus privately at night, presumably because he did not want to be seen visiting the controversial Christ by his colleagues. Nicodemus was a member of the Israelite ruling council called the Sanhedrin. He was also a Pharisee (a member of the most religious sect of Judaism) living in Jerusalem. Pharisees believed in the truth of Scripture, the existence of the invisible spirit realm and of angels, and the miraculous. This man, Nicodemus, attempted to live strictly according to the Law of Moses, besides the traditions Pharisaism added to God's Word. He worked to follow all ceremonial law and religious observance. Christ would astound him by explaining that being born again and not good works would be sufficient for Nicodemus' salvation.

When Nicodemus visited Christ, he said that "we [Pharisees] know that you [Jesus Christ] are a teacher who has come to us from God" (John 3:2). Nicodemus understood that miracles performed by Jesus were by the authority and power of God. Yet when Jesus replied to Nicodemus, He spoke of the need for even the ultra-religious Nicodemus to be "born again." Jesus, being in very nature God, knew the sin in men's hearts (John 2:25). It is important to note that Nicodemus, though by today's standards extraordinarily religious, was uncertain of receiving eternal life in Heaven!

What does the phrase "born again" (used so loosely today in popular culture), specifically mean? Nicodemus asked Jesus, "How can a man be born when he is old? Surely he cannot enter a second time into His mother's womb to be born!" (John 3:4). With an illustration of the new, spiritual birth (being born again from Heaven), Jesus explained. The first birth is a natural, or physical, birth. To be born again is to be given eternal life by God through the Holy Spirit. Jesus explained that the Holy Spirit (the third person of the Godhead) is powerful and unseen—like the wind itself. To "believe" in Jesus Christ is to trust (a one-time act performed in sincerity) in Christ's taking our sins upon Himself through His death on the cross and His subsequent resurrection and appearance before many witnesses.

> When I came to you, brothers, I did not come with eloquence or superior wisdom as I proclaimed to you the testimony about God. For I resolved to know nothing while I was with you except Jesus Christ and him crucified. 1 Corinthians 2:1–2

When Paul brought the good news to the people of Corinth, he proclaimed his testimony about God in simple terms. The good news is that the wrath of God is averted when the sinner becomes born again and is transformed by God into a saint. Christ called out on the cross: "It is finished!" He had come to do the will of God by making a finished and complete payment for man's sin. Jesus had fulfilled the purpose of His coming.

Jesus, before going to His cross, prayed:

"Father, if you are willing, take this cup from me; yet not my will, but yours be done." Luke 22:2

It was the Father's will that Jesus drink the cup of the Father's wrath. To be born again is to be made spiritually alive through the acceptance of Christ's payment made for the penalty of sin (spiritual death), paid in full on the cross. When we accept salvation through trusting in Christ, we are at that specific time sealed by the Holy Spirit unto the day of redemption (Ephesians 4:30) and are reconciled to the Father (2 Corinthians 5:18–19). Our body has become a temple of the Holy Spirit (1 Corinthians 6:19). The born-again Christian is someone who has trusted in Christ's death and resurrection, and they have assurance from that time forward that they will have eternal life in Heaven.

Now we have established a scriptural basis for a plain definition of God's wrath—the context is the eternal state of separation from God due to sin. We now shall examine the term "completion of God's wrath." The completion of God's wrath as written in Revelation and elsewhere is subtly different, a one-time event that takes place during a highly specified period of time. Scripture clearly informs us when God's wrath shall be completed, and a difficulty for many interpreters has rested in assessing the following statement:

> I saw . . . seven angels with the seven last plagues—last because
> with them God's wrath is completed. Revelation 15:7

God's wrath is completed with the outpouring of the bowl judgments during the tribulation of seven years and not before the seven years begin; it is specifically stated that the pouring out of the seven golden bowls filled with the wrath of God upon the earth *completes* God's wrath. This event takes place directly after the "first harvest of the earth." (See Revelation 14:1–16.)

The Wheat, Barley, and Grape Harvests

As mentioned in the previous chapter, in line with the spring harvest calendar, Jesus fulfilled the spring cycle of biblical festivals. He rose from the dead on the Feast of Firstfruits, for example. This festival was held at the start of the barley harvest. The Church received the Holy Spirit at Pentecost, in another instance. This festival, fifty days after the Feast of Firstfruits, included a day of Firstfruits, but this second harvest celebrated the beginning of the *wheat*, not the *barley*, harvest. Jesus used the wheat harvest to symbolize the rapture of the Church (John 4:35).

Therefore, the "harvest of the earth," which is a wheat harvest as described in Revelation 14, is followed immediately by the harvest symbolized by grapes. (The end of the wheat harvest is followed by the grape harvest.) Thus, the removing of the Church from the earth (wheat harvest) is followed soon after by the punishment of the wicked on the earth (the trampling out of the vintage of the grapes). (See Revelation 14:20.)

> "Immediately after the distress of those days, the sun will be darkened, and the moon will not give its light; the stars will fall from the sky and the heavenly bodies will be shaken." Matthew 24:29

In the verses that follow this description of distressing signs in sky, the sign of the Son of Man appears in the sky. In Luke's gospel, we are again told that there will be signs in the Sun, Moon, and stars.

> "When these things begin to take place, stand up and lift your heads, because your redemption is drawing near." Luke 21:28

The Bible is so very capable of encouraging and informing believers! According to the words of Jesus, the Church on Earth will see the heavens shaken. Scripture tells us that after the "distress of those days" the heavens will be shaken and the sign of the Son of Man will appear in the sky. (The earth, certainly, will be shaken, and the heavenly bodies will seem to do so from the vantage of observers on Earth; see 2 Peter 3, for instance.) When we see these things (the shaking and distress) occur, we are to look up into the heavens because our literal redemption in Christ is near.

The elect Christian believers are not subject to God's wrath but will remain on Earth until the outpouring of God's wrath on the earth—a view common to all *pre-millennial* interpretations of the rapture. The saints of God will be persecuted and many martyred before the elect are raptured in this pre-wrath view.

During this time of tribulation, those who obey God's commandments and hold to the testimony of Jesus will suffer greatly during the reign of the Antichrist (Revelation 12:17). A fearful warning of those coming days:

> "The king will do as he pleases. He will exalt and magnify himself . . . He will be successful until the time of wrath is completed . . ." Daniel 11:36

The outpouring of God's wrath signals the end of the power of the Antichrist. The Church is removed from the earth and the wicked suffer as a result of the seven last plagues.

Now the "seventh trumpet" is sounded just prior to the time of the completion of God's wrath:

> The seventh angel sounded His trumpet . . . and the twenty-four elders . . . fell on their faces and worshipped God saying: "We give thanks to you, LORD God . . . because you . . . have begun to reign . . . your wrath has come . . . the time has come for rewarding your servants the prophets and your saints . . ." Revelation 11:15–18

The completion of God's wrath occurs during a specific time period. It commences at the seventh trumpet. The seven trumpets will be the topic of our next chapter.

Summary of Chapter Three

- There is a biblical distinction made between "wrath" on those who reject Christ and are condemned to Hell and "the completion of God's wrath," which is an outpouring of plague-like judgments on an unrepentant world. An individual escapes the "wrath of God upon sinners" through becoming born again by trusting in Jesus Christ's death and resurrection. Born-again individuals will escape "God's wrath upon the earth" at the rapture.
- The completion of God's wrath occurs at the last (seventh) trumpet of Revelation.
- The seven festivals of Leviticus 23 are to be fulfilled in Christ, four of them having been completed already in at Christ's First Advent. The last three feasts and other references to Christ's return will be presented throughout this book.

Chapter 4

The Seventh Trumpet Sounds at the Rapture?

"But in the days when the seventh angel is about to sound His trumpet, the mystery of God will be accomplished, just as he announced to His servants the prophets."

—Revelation 10:7

People sent by God to deliver God's message to an individual or specific group of persons were known as God's prophets. Their prophetic utterances were enscripturated (the Word of God as spoken through the prophets, written and verified as Scripture). An examination of prophetic Scripture affords us a depth of understanding related to the terms "seventh trumpet" and "the mystery of God." To accurately interpret the meaning of verse of Revelation 10:7, we need the context of why and when trumpets were sounded in Israel and in the ancient world.

The names for two distinct types of wind instruments used by the nation of Israel have been translated in our English Bible as the word *trumpet*. One type was a silver trumpet (cf. Numbers 10:1–10) and the other, a ram's horn, commonly called a "*shofar*," blown to commemorate the sacrifice of Abraham.

On the first day of the seventh biblical month of Tishri, Israel was to have a day of rest, a sacred assembly, commemorated with blasts on a silver trumpet (Leviticus 23:23–25; Numbers 29:1–6). This Feast of Trumpets is known today as the Jewish New Year, or Rosh HaShona (literally, "head of the year"). Rosh HaShona is the first day of the civil calendar and was first celebrated when the Jewish people returned to Israel after seventy years' captivity in Babylon. [Author's Note: Unlike the civil calendar, the first month of the religious calendar is the spring month of Nisan (or Abib) as ordained by God in Exodus 12:2. The first three Levitical festivals take place in the month of Nisan. The last three festivals of the book of Leviticus take place in the fall month of Tishri.]

During Rosh HaShona, Genesis 22 is read during the synagogue service. This is the account of Abraham, tested in his faith and found obedient. Abraham was commanded by God to sacrifice his son Isaac as a burnt offering; as Abraham lifted his knife to slay Isaac, the angel of the Lord called to him from Heaven:

"Do not lay a hand on the boy . . . do not do anything to him. Now I know that you fear God, because you have not withheld from me your son, your only son." Genesis 22:12

Abraham and Isaac soon saw a ram caught by its horns in a thicket. Abraham sacrificed the ram in place of his son. A ram's horn, or *shofar*, is blown during the Feast of Trumpets in remembrance of the deliverance of Isaac.

A burnt offering such as Abraham's ram acts as both a voluntary act of worship and an atonement offering. Why? The life of a creature is in its blood (Leviticus 17:11). The blood of a sacrificial animal is sprinkled upon an altar, serving as a temporary covering for sin. Blood sacrifice is also a picture of the sacrifice of Jesus Christ making permanent atonement. Animal blood can not permanently remove sin. An animal's life is not equivalent to the life of a human being, for humans are the only creatures created in the image and likeness of God (Genesis 1:27).

God preserved the account of the history of Israel as an example for the Church (1 Corinthians 10:6). An event in the natural realm is afforded to us first so we can next develop our spiritual understanding (cf. 1 Corinthians 15:44–49). Genesis 22, therefore, paints an important principle of New Testament Scripture for us:

"God so loved the world that he gave His one and only Son . . ."
John 3:16a

When Isaac saw the fire and wood for the burnt offering, he asked his father, "Where is the lamb?" At that time, a *ram, not a lamb*, was provided. The place where this scene transpired was called "Jehovah *Jireh*" (the Lord will provide). God provided Himself as the lamb in the person of His Son. Nearly two millennia after Isaac's search for a lamb, John the Baptist was standing in the Jordan River when he saw Jesus and said:

"Look, the Lamb of God who takes away the sin of the world!"
John 1:29b

The Law of Moses stipulated penalties for injury to another person: a life for a life, an eye for an eye taken, a tooth broken for another's tooth, and so forth. (See Exodus 21:23–24.) If Jesus were but a man, His sacrifice under the law could pay the debt of but one other person. Jesus, however, who is fully both the Son of Man and the Son of God (Romans 1:3–4), is divine and of infinite worth. He was able to lay down His life as a ransom for many (Matthew 20:28; Mark 10:45).

By faith, Abraham, when God tested him, offered Isaac as a sacrifice. He who had received the promises was about to sacrifice his one and only son, though God had said to him, "It is through Isaac that your offspring will be reckoned" (Hebrews 11:17–18).

Abraham had another son, Ishmael, by his wife's Egyptian handmaiden. The phrase, "one and only son," is to emphasize the fact that only Isaac was the son of promise and rightful heir (Genesis 15:4). Abraham had purposed in his heart to carry out God's command and offer up Isaac as an offering for sin. How then, could Abraham sacrifice his son, and yet, God fulfill His promise that through Isaac would Abraham's offspring be reckoned? Abraham reasoned that God could raise the dead, and figuratively speaking, he did receive Isaac back from death. (See Hebrews 11:19.)

Abraham reasoned that God could raise the dead, and, symbolically, Isaac "resurrected." This account gives us a prophetic picture of Christ's atoning death and resurrection. Seven hundred years before the incarnation of Christ (God being manifested in the form of human flesh), the prophet speaks of the ministry, death, and resurrection of God's suffering servant, Messiah:

> Yet it was the LORD's will to crush him and cause him to suffer, and though the LORD makes His life a guilt offering, he will see His offspring and prolong His days, and the will of the LORD will prosper in His hand. Isaiah 53:10

The blowing of the shofar, therefore, not only commemorates the testing of Abraham's faith, but is also associated with the resurrection of the righteous (1 Thessalonians 4:15–16; Revelation 20:4).

Israel was a divided kingdom after the reign of Solomon. The Northern Kingdom, Samaria, had been taken into captivity by Assyria (722–721 B.C.). The people of the Southern Kingdom, Judah, were taken into exile over a century later. After a period of seventy years, the exiles returned to Jerusalem in Judah and again began to offer burnt offerings to the Lord. The daily sacrifice commenced on the first day of the seventh month. (See Ezra 3:6.) Psalm 90:10 begins: "The length of our days is seventy years . . ." Symbolically, the nation was spiritually dead (that is, separated from God) for a "lifetime" of seventy years.

When the exiles left sinful Babylon (Babylon is a biblical type or "picture" of our sinful world), the nation returned to the worship and the presence of the Lord in Israel. This picture of the resurrection of the people of God took place on the Feast of Trumpets.

Figuratively speaking, as discussed above, Isaac rose from the dead. He is a type of Christ, the firstfruits of the resurrection of the righteous (1 Corinthians 15:23). Centuries after the testing of Abraham, the Jews returned to the land from seventy years of captivity. Figuratively speaking, Israel (a type of the Church) is raised from the dead as well.

These two events, the "raising" of Isaac and the return from captivity in Babylon, which foreshadow resurrection, are both associated with the Feast of Trumpets.

Let us look more closely at the resurrection of believers:

> According to the LORD's own word, we will tell you that we who are still alive, who are left till the coming of the LORD, will certainly not precede those who have fallen asleep. For the LORD himself will come down from heaven, with a loud command, with the voice of the archangel and with the trumpet call of God and the dead in Christ will rise first. 1 Thessalonians 4:15–16

There will be born-again believers in Christ who will be physically alive at His coming. First, those believers who are "asleep in Christ" (who have died physically but are spiritually alive!) will resurrect from the dead to new bodies. Then those believers still alive on Earth will be together with them in the clouds to meet the Lord in the air above the earth (1 Thessalonians 4:17). This rapture takes place immediately after the resurrection of the righteous dead *at the sounding of the trumpet call of God* (Matthew 24:31).

What are other purposes of the silver trumpet? The silver trumpet was sounded in Israel on a frequent basis. The command of the Lord to Moses concerning the fashioning of the two silver trumpets is found in Numbers 10:1–10. They were used for calling the community together and having the camps of the people set out upon their journeys. When both silver trumpets were sounded, the whole community was to assemble before Moses at the Tent of Meeting (the tabernacle, or pitched tent, where God met with Israel). Both trumpets signaled that all God's chosen people were to meet with God at His appointed time and place (Exodus 29:43; Numbers 10:3).

The sounding of the trumpets was for the assembling of the people and unto marching, battle and festivals as well:

"Also at your times of rejoicing . . . your appointed feasts and New Moon festivals . . . you are to sound the trumpets . . ." Numbers 10:10a

Note that at the new moon, the shofar was blown as well:

Sound the ram's horn at the New Moon, and when the moon is full, on the day of our Feast . . . Psalm 81:3

At the new moon (when the Moon is darkened on the first day of the month), *both the silver trumpets and the ram's horn* were to be sounded. Rosh HaShona, the Jewish New Year, takes place on the first day of the seventh month. In the seventh month, the New Moon Festival coincides with the Feast of Trumpets.

"And he will send His angels with a loud trumpet call, and they will gather His elect from the four winds, from one end of the heavens to the other." Matthew 24:31

The silver trumpets announce the gathering of God's people before His presence. The blowing of the shofar is associated with the resurrection of the righteous. Both the silver trumpets and the ram's horn are sounded on the first day of the first month at the new moon. The second time during the ceremonial calendar year that the trumpets sound is on the first day of the second month, and so the *seventh time* the trumpets are sounded is on the first day of the *seventh* month at Rosh HaShona—The Feast of Trumpets!

I believe that there is strong evidence to support a position that at Rosh HaShona on the Hebrew calendar the seventh angel will someday sound his Revelation trumpet (Revelation 10:7). Jesus Christ resurrected on the Feast of Firstfruits. The Holy Spirit came down at Pentecost (Feast of Weeks). It logically can be deduced that in future the elect will be raptured on the Feast of Trumpets. (As will be explained, this is not "date setting" as is admonished against in the Scripture, as in Matthew 24:36.) Further evidence for this doctrinal position is presented in the following chapter as we investigate the "mystery of God."

Summary of Chapter Four

- There are two types of trumpets sounded in Scripture:

    1. A silver trumpet, announcing rest from works for the people for a solemn assembly before the Lord or a battle assembly.
    2. A ram's horn, or shofar, blown to commemorate Abraham's sacrifice of Isaac and symbolic of the resurrection of true believers.

- At the New Moon festival each month of the Jewish calendar, both the ram's horn and silver trumpet are to be sounded—the seventh such occurrence of each year is on the Feast of Trumpets also known as the Jewish New Year (Rosh HaShona). I would not hesitate to assign the "seventh trumpet" of Revelation to occur at the New Moon festival of the seventh month (Rosh HaShona) for reasons outlined in the remainder of this book.

Chapter 5

* *

The Mystery of God: So, What Is the Big Mystery?

My purpose is that they may be encouraged in heart and united in love, so that they may have the full riches of complete understanding, in order that they may know the mystery of God, namely Christ, in whom are hidden all the treasures of wisdom and knowledge.

—Colossians 2:3

The term "mystery," as utilized in Scripture, does not describe information that is withheld, but rather, a biblical truth that people could not fathom for themselves without receiving divine revelation.

Colossians 2:3 is from Paul's inspiring letter to faithful brothers in Christ at Colosse. The Colossian church in Western Asia was in close proximity to the church at Laodicea, a lukewarm church and one of the seven churches specifically addressed in the book of Revelation. Paul's message was intended, of course, for the churches of Colosse and Laodicea and all of those in Christ who would read His letter. His desire is that those of the faith would love one another, producing unity in the body of believers.

United Truth and the Life (John 14:6)

If knowledge is the knowing of true facts and truth, and in Christ is the hidden source in love, we can dispel the lukewarm attitudes that plagued the Laodicean church and fully comprehend the mystery of God, namely Christ. In Christ is hidden all knowledge! Jesus is the way and the all of wisdom; wisdom being the correct application of truth unto life and benefit, then it was correctly prophesied that:

> A shoot will come up from the stump of Jesse; from His roots a Branch will bear fruit. The Spirit of the LORD will rest on him—the Spirit of wisdom and understanding . . . Isaiah 11:1–2a

Now the "Jesse" mentioned above was the father of King David. One title of the Messiah is the Righteous Branch, born of the royal line of David. The prophet Micah foretold that the ruler over Israel would be born in Bethlehem, the ancestral home of David's clan, yet whose origins are from ancient times, that is, eternity (Micah 5:2). Jesus was born in Bethlehem and is the eternal God as well.

Luke's gospel testifies that Jesus traveled to Nazareth, where he had been raised by Joseph and Mary, and went to the local synagogue (Luke 4:16). Jesus was a Jew from the tribe of Judah, and so then of David, but He was known as a Nazarene. And a righteous branch? The Hebrew word, "*nezer*" is translated as "branch." We have play on words between "righteous branch" and "Nazareth" in the Hebrew, with both pronunciations quite similar. Jesus' genealogy testified to His Messiahship. The righteous branch was rooted in the royal family tree of David. (See Matthew 1:1–17; Luke 3:21–38.)

Matthew's genealogy of the righteous branch begins with Abraham, patriarch of the Jewish people, and traces the legal descent of the house of David by naming heirs to the throne. This account ends with Joseph, the legal, adoptive father of Jesus.

Luke's genealogy, in contrast, starts with Joseph as son-in-law of Heli, Mary's father. Luke traces the line of Mary, Jesus' direct blood relative. This "natural line" is traced to Adam and Eve. Jesus is both the legal (Joseph's line) and natural (Mary's line) heir to the throne of Israel.

Jesus read aloud during the service at the synagogue in Nazareth as recorded in Luke. This traditional reading was an honor and privilege, as before the invention of the printing press, few people owned the Scriptures. Unlike the Bibles of today, when pages can be turned at speed or searched through instantly on the Internet to find key terms, the handwritten scrolls of Jesus' day were ceremonially unveiled and unrolled carefully. Each Sabbath a particular portion was read from the *Torah* (also called the "Five Books of Moses," the "Pentateuch," or "the Law"), plus a particular portion was read from the *Haftorah* (the Prophets and Writings, the remaining books of the Old Testament). Following the close of the Torah cycle of readings through the year, the entire scroll was re-rolled; the same selected Scripture portions being read again in the same order for each Sabbath the following year, a liturgical calendar of Bible readings.

When Jesus read from the scroll of Isaiah, the particular passage would only be available only one Sabbath each year for a public reading. Every synagogue worldwide would read the same portion on the same date. It was no coincidence that Jesus read from Isaiah 61:1–2 during His reading. Fulfilling this Scripture portion, Jesus proclaimed that He was the Messiah, anointed to preach the gospel, because the Holy Spirit rested upon Him. (See Luke 4:18–21.)

In Christ, the righteous branch, is hidden all treasures of wisdom and understanding. He is the mystery of God! Jesus Christ of

Nazareth is both a name and a title: "The Anointed Branch Who Saves His People from Their Sin" (Matthew 1:21). The Lord Jesus Christ is the embodiment of all truth, wisdom, and understanding.

Look at the Revelation mystery of God for a comparison to Christ as the mystery of God:

> "But in the days when the seventh angel is about to sound His trumpet, the mystery of God will be accomplished, just as he announced to His servants the prophets." Revelation 10:7

The mystery of God is Christ, in whom are hidden all the treasures of wisdom and knowledge. At the seventh trumpet the mystery of God will be accomplished with a successful completion.

What is Meant by Jesus, the Mystery of God Completed?

> And He is the head of the body, the church; He is the beginning and the firstborn from among the dead, so that in everything He might have the supremacy. Colossians 1:18

For the mystery of God to be accomplished, the Body of Christ, the Church, must be raptured to join with Christ. At the rapture, Christ will be united forever with His church (1 Thessalonians 4:17). The union of the Head and the Body of the Church will accomplish the mystery of God. The firstborn from among the dead, Christ the firstfruits, or first resurrected from death, will be joined with the rest of the wheat harvest at the coming resurrection of the righteous. Christians may take great comfort in these words:

> "At that time they will see the Son of Man coming in a cloud with power and great glory. When these things begin to take

place, stand up and lift your heads, because your redemption is drawing near." Luke 21:27–28

Look, he is coming with the clouds, and every eye will see him, even those who pierced him; and all of the peoples of the earth will mourn because of him so shall it be! Amen. Revelation 1:7

What Are the "Clouds" Accompanying the Mystery of God?

Hebrews gives us insight on this important question. Hebrews 11 is well known as the Bible's great chapter on the faith of the saints. Many examples of acts of faith by men and women who lived during Old Testament times are cited in this chapter. In reference to these heroes and heroines who lived by faith, chapter twelve begins:

Therefore, since we are surrounded by such a great cloud of witnesses . . . Hebrews 12:1a

The biblical terms "cloud" or "clouds" represent the souls of men and women who have died in Christ. To be absent from the body is to be present with the Lord for those who are righteous by faith. Paul declared that he desired to "depart and be with Christ, which is better by far" (Philippians 1:23). Jesus spoke of the cloud, saying:

"Immediately after the distress of those days, the sun will be darkened, and the moon will not give its light; the stars will fall from the sky, and the heavenly bodies will be shaken . . . at that time they will see the Son of Man coming in a cloud with power and great glory. When these things begin to take place, stand up and lift your heads, because your redemption is drawing near." Luke 21:27–28

Those of the elect who have not been martyred during the events of Revelation will be encouraged to stand firm in the faith. "For their sake those days of great distress will be shortened." They will see wonders in the heaven above and signs on the earth beneath (Acts 2:19). The elect will see the sign of the coming of the Son of Man, perhaps a sign of the cross, in the sky. At that time, many of the persecuted Christians will be imprisoned (Revelation 13:10). As they lie on their face or kneel in prayer, the very shaking of the heavens will rouse them. Those who have remained faithful will stand up and lift their heads high, strengthened to know their redemption is at hand.

> In Him we have redemption through His blood, the forgiveness of sins, in accordance with the riches of God's grace that he lavished on us with all wisdom and understanding. Ephesians 1:7–8

The elect in Christ already have redemption (have been purchased and reconciled to God the Father to date) through the atoning blood of Jesus Christ. He paid the price in full. Christians' sins have been forgiven. We have been regenerated and are partakers of the divine nature itself (2 Peter 1:4), though our sinful bodies are corrupting (1 Corinthians 15:42).

> "Stand up and lift up your heads, because your redemption is drawing near." Luke 21:28b

Note carefully that Luke 21 does not read "lift up your heads, because your *redeemer* is drawing near" but "because your *redemption*" is drawing near. What type of redemption could it be that living saints, who have every spiritual blessing at present, have not already acquired?

Not only so, but we ourselves, who have the firstfruits of the Spirit, groan inwardly as we await eagerly for our adoption as sons, the redemption of our bodies. Romans 8:23

During the time of the Great Tribulation (a period of time I understand to be the second half of Daniel's seventieth week, 1260 days in duration), living saints have been marked in Christ with a seal, the Holy Spirit (Ephesians 1:13–14). They persevere as they eagerly await the Redeemer to bring redemption of their bodies. At the sounding of the trumpet by the seventh angel, the mystery of God is accomplished, namely Christ, as He joins finally to His Church. His bride (the Church), has made herself ready (Revelation 19:7b). Having been purified and readied by the cleansing fire of persecution, the Church is raptured to meet the Lord in the air.

Adam and Eve as a Living picture of Christ as Redeemer

As Eve was taken from Adam's side (Genesis 2:21–23), God created them male and female (Genesis 1:27), yet man and woman are to unite as one flesh (Genesis 2:24). Eve was taken from Adam's side. When Jesus hung on the cross, He was pierced in *His side* with a spear, and blood and water poured forth. The Church was symbolically birthed from His side—purchased by His blood and filled with His Spirit (living water). The Church, taken from and with the Lord's side, unites more completely in Christ in God's Spirit at the marriage of the Lamb, following the rapture.

My understanding is that those who hold to the pre-tribulation concept of end time events misinterpret Revelation 1:7, which clearly states that "he is coming with the clouds, and every eye will see him . . ."

The Lord certainly will come with the clouds but there is a misunderstanding of the meaning of the term "clouds." Many pre-tribulation teachers equate the term "clouds" with the glorified

Church and state that the Lord must first come *for the Church* before He can *come back with the Church*. They contend that this verse supports their view that the rapture takes place a full seven years before the Lord returns to the earth to set up His kingdom.

How can the term "clouds" be a metaphor for the raptured Church when the rapture is comprised of the resurrected righteous *and those who are still alive at His coming?* (See 1 Thessalonians 4:15.) At the rapture, *both* categories of saints will possess immortal bodies. He is *"coming with (already alongside) the clouds . . ."* Do we have a distinct biblical term identifying only those righteous who have gone on to be with the Lord, those who have died? Yes! The *"cloud of witnesses"* of Hebrews 12:1. The "clouds" are clearly the disembodied souls of the saints. He does not have to come for the clouds in the dramatic prophecy of Revelation 1:7, as in the pre-tribulation view, because they are *already* with Him.

This leads us to the subject of the next chapter: Although their righteous souls are with Him (Revelation 6:9), their bodies are still in the grave awaiting glorification (God's transformation of our corruptible flesh into a spirit body). This mystery is the subject of our next chapter.

Summary of Chapter Five

- The mystery of God is found (always!) in the glorious Jesus Christ. (See Colossians 2:3.)

    o   This mystery is completed powerfully in the marriage of Christ to His Church: Christ was pierced in His side and John recorded the witness of the blood and water, which flowed as a testimony to the world; this is also a powerful echo of Adam's vital joining to Eve, mother of all the living.

- The correct interpretation of the debated word *clouds* is essential to a rapture understanding.

    o Scripture seems to indicate that the "cloud of witnesses" is saints who have died and uses the more general and plural term "clouds" to connote both living and dead believers at once.

- A key verse for many pre-tribulation scholars is Revelation 1:7, taken to indicate the rapture is to "fetch" the Church before the tribulation begins, yet this verse states that instead *the clouds are already with* Christ.

Chapter **6**

"We Will Not All Sleep"

It is essential that Scripture studies be undertaken in their correct context. We need to understand the culture, customs, and belief system of those to whom the letter to the Corinthians was intended, to best interpret these two epistles properly.

Paul, an apostle and a founder of the Corinthian church, wrote:

> To the church of God in Corinth, to those sanctified in Christ Jesus and called to be holy, together with those everywhere who call on the name of our LORD Jesus Christ—their LORD and ours."
> 1 Corinthians 1:1–2

> Listen, I tell you a mystery: We will not all sleep, but we will all be changed—in a flash, in the twinkling of an eye, at the last trumpet. For the trumpet will sound, the dead will be raised imperishable, and we will be changed. 1 Corinthians 15:51–52

"*We will* [all] *be changed*" refers only to all of *those sanctified in Christ Jesus and called to be holy,* that is, biblical Christians. Did you know that to be sanctified in Christ is distinct from calling oneself a Christian or holding membership in a local church? Sanctification in Christ signifies consecration in Christ for the born-again believer and connotes being set apart from the world and bearing righteous fruit—holiness—following conversion. The message of this Corinthian mystery of chapter fifteen is intended for all true believers in Christ Jesus.

When the final trumpet of Revelation sounds, it will announce the gathering together of the saints to meet the Lord in the air. It will be the final trumpet call for the Church! No longer will a trumpet sound to gather God's congregation together in His presence. Believers who are alive at His Second Coming will be together forever with those who have died in Christ. Following the rapture, those who comprise the true Church will be with the Lord forever. (See 1 Thessalonians 4:17.)

What Do the Scriptures Mean by "Asleep In Christ?"

To better understand the concept of dying in Christ (called "falling asleep in Christ"), we will examine the account of Jesus raising Lazarus from the dead.

> "[Jesus said] Our friend Lazarus has fallen asleep; but I am going there to wake him up." His disciples replied, 'LORD, if he sleeps, he will get better.' Jesus had been speaking of His death, but His disciples thought he meant natural sleep." John 11:11–13

Jesus had intentionally delayed responding to the plea of Mary and Martha, the sisters of Lazarus, who had sent this message to Jesus: "Lord, the one you love is sick" (John 11:3). When Jesus finally arrived in Bethany, Lazarus had been interred in a tomb for four days. After the third day of death, the body decays and corrupts at an accelerated rate. (Jesus, unlike Lazarus, rose on the third day before "corruption" set in fully. When Jesus resurrected on the third day, prophecy was fulfilled that the Holy One of the LORD would not see decay [see Psalm 16:10]).

Although Jesus allowed the sickly Lazarus to die, it was not an act motivated by lack of compassion—Jesus wept for Lazarus' passing and the grief of his family and friends (John 11:35). Jesus was to demonstrate in power that He is the resurrection and the life (John 11:25a). Jesus raised a stinking corpse to life again! (See John 11:39.)

Jesus loved Lazarus fully. Lazarus was not separated from God (spiritually dead), although he indeed physically died. Lazarus was raised from the dead in a mortal body, to physically die again soon after at the hands of Jesus' enemies.

At the last trumpet, all of the righteous dead (Christians called "asleep in Christ" in the New Testament) will be raised with imperishable, brand new bodies. At the last trumpet, all those sanctified in Christ, both the then-resurrected saints and those alive at His coming, will be changed—in an instant, in the twinkling of an eye.

> But someone may ask, "How are the dead raised? With what kind of body will they come?" 1 Corinthians 15:35

Paul asks this rhetorical question in order to prepare his readers to receive a spiritual principle and provide a natural example to draw upon. In the natural realm, a person who desires to grow wheat does not sow a full stalk of wheat but merely a seed. When the seed sprouts into a plant, the plant is quite unlike the seed from which it has sprouted. Paul's analogy compares a person's buried and dead body to a dead, buried, and germinated seed. When a person is resurrected, the new spiritual body is to be quite unlike the seed, the physical body, which was "planted" in the grave.

What Is the "True Resurrection?"

What does that jargon term mean?

> So it will be with the resurrection of the dead. The body that is sown is perishable, it is raised imperishable; it is sown in dishonor, it is raised in glory; it is sown in weakness, it is raised in power; it is sown a natural body, it is raised a spiritual body. 1 Corinthians 15:42–44

The body that is sown (buried in death) had been born in dishonor and sin and sown in corruptibility. God's creation epitomized was the creation of man in His own image—now fallen into dishonor. "God saw all he had made, and it was very good . . ." (Genesis 1:31a).

> Therefore, just as sin entered the world through one man, and death through sin, and in this way death came to all men, because all sinned. Romans 5:12

Originally, man, and man's created body was "very good." Due to sin, the body of man is currently under the curse of corruption unto death. But for individuals receiving the gift of God's grace through salvation, their bodies will ultimately be raised in power, new, imperishable, and glorified.

> According to the LORD's own word, we tell you that we who are still alive; who are left till the coming of the LORD, will certainly not precede those who have fallen asleep. 1 Thessalonians 4:15

Those who have died in Christ will be raised in resurrection power. Their new spiritual bodies will be united with their souls (mind, will, and emotions). Man was created in the image of the triune God, created with three distinct aspects that comprise his nature.

So God created man in His own image, in the image of God he
created him; male and female he created them. Genesis 1:27

Are there biblical distinctions to be made between a person's
"spirit" and "soul?"

God is spirit. John 4:24

The body of man was formed from the dust of the ground
(physical elements). The spirit of man dwells in a physical body.
Man also has the ability to think, feel, and act according to God's
will or his own will. God created man in His image, and God is a
spirit being. God created the spirit of man, which makes man a
unique creation.

The LORD God formed the man from the dust of the ground and
breathed into His nostrils the breath of life, and the man became
a living being. Genesis 1:7

The souls of men consist of their minds, wills, and emotions.
Although our bodies change substantially as they grow into matu-
rity, we maintain a stream of consciousness and self-awareness.
Paul wrote these final remarks in a letter to the Christians of
Thessalonica:

May God himself, the God of peace sanctify you through and
through. May your whole spirit, soul and body be kept blame-
less at the coming of our LORD Jesus Christ. 1 Thessalonians 5:23

When Adam disobeyed God, he died spiritually. Adam's sin
separated him from the presence of God. Adam was placed under
a curse and expelled from Eden. For Adam's children, noble think-
ing became darkened due to sin and the focus from protection and

provision for the self and others to a selfish and self-centered struggle. Due to "spiritual fallout" on the nature of Adam's progeny, the souls of men slowly perish in corruption until the moment of physical death, unless they are born again through Christ.

At the moment of spiritual rebirth for the new Christian, a person is reconciled to God and receives eternal life through Christ—and although a person is reconciled to God for eternity at the moment of regeneration, neither *soul* nor *perishing physical body* is fully perfected. As a person grows in the grace and knowledge of Christ, however, by studying the Scriptures, seeking the LORD in prayer, and participating in private devotionals and corporate worship, his mind grows to be wonderfully renewed (Romans 12:2). This lifelong process affecting the heart, mind, and emotions is known as "sanctification." The believer's will becomes more closely conformed toward the image of Christ (Romans 8:29). Finally, at the coming of the Lord, the body of the true Christian is perfected as an actual new and imperishable physical body hardly comprehensible to our finite understanding.

> We all, like sheep have gone astray each of us has turned to His own way; and the LORD has laid on him the iniquity of us all. Isaiah 53:6

> God made him who had no sin to be sin for us, so that in him we might become the righteousness of God. 2 Corinthians 5:21

On the cross, Jesus—both God and man—took our sin upon Himself. When the sin of the world was laid on Him, the Godhead was torn apart, and Jesus died spiritually. [Author's note: I recognize that many may balk at the concept of the immutable and only God being torn apart to pay the price of atonement. It does seems likely that Jesus first died spiritually before He died a physical death; but to recognize His physical death of "one man for a sacrifice for one man" as Christians and not consider a true, world-atoning spiritual death seems to echo heretical and Gnostic sentiments, dividing the physical from the spiritual in any man's or Jesus' true nature. We would believe immediately upon first impulse that God cannot "die" (cease to exist). But if God died spiritually in Jesus on the cross, and Jesus was spiritually separated from the Father, how horrific and absolute His price for salvation! How much more readily we might embrace the notion of unlimited atonement for the one who takes away "all the sins of the world!"]

His horrific separation from the Father is why Jesus Christ cried out:

> "'Eloi, Eloi, lama sabachthani?" which means, "My God, my God, why have you forsaken me?" Matthew 27:46b

For the only time in all of eternity, God the Father turned His back to God the Son. Jesus bore the full cup of God's wrath and was separated from the Father. Jesus cried aloud, "It is finished!" (John 19:30). He had come to do the Father's will by solving (in what is still worldwide today a mostly misunderstood triumph), the ancient problem of evil. Finally, He died a physical death on the cross. It was the Father's will to crush Him and cause Him to suffer. It was the Father's will also to make the Son's life a guilt offering for sin (Isaiah 53:10). Jesus suffered, died, and then rose again in victory!

> We believe that Jesus died and rose again and so we believe that God will bring with Jesus those who have fallen asleep in him. 1 Thessalonians 4:14

At the sounding of the seventh trumpet (I believe) the dead in Christ will resurrect. Any born-again believers who are alive at

His coming will be transformed together with the resurrected righteous saints to meet the Lord in the air. "And so we will be with the LORD forever" (1 Thessalonians 4:17b).

> Blessed and holy are those who have part in the first resurrection. The second death has no power over them . . . Revelation 20:6a

Those who have been born again were once separate from God, due to sin. Biblical Christians have had two births, physical, or *natural* birth, and a spiritual, or *supernatural* birth.

> Yet to all who received him, to those who believed in His name, he gave the right to become children of God—children born not of natural descent, nor of human decision, or a husband's will, but born of God. John 1:13

What does the book of Revelation mean by a "first" resurrection (above)? Those who have part in the *first resurrection*, which is the resurrection of those dead who are "asleep in Christ," will not experience the *second death*. The second death is the penultimate fate awaiting those who reject Jesus Christ.

Those who were not part of the first resurrection (the unrighteous dead not saved by Christ) will be raised to life for the purpose of standing before the "great white throne" of God for excoriating judgment (Revelation 20:11). The teeming dead (whose names are not recorded in the book of life) before the throne of God will be judged for degree of punishment according to what they have done while "in the body" during their lifetime. Eternal, living consignment to the lake of fire, coming after physical death on Earth, is thus the *second death* (Revelation 20:14). Multitudes who have experienced natural birth but who died in their sins separated from God are raised to life at the *second, not the first, resurrection.* They stand in the awesome and glorious presence of Almighty God and will be cast from His presence forever—the second death of eternal separation from God.

> "They will throw them into the fiery furnace, where there will be weeping and gnashing of teeth." Matthew 13:42

A commonly used slogan emphasizing this fact is the following: "Be born once [on Earth] and die twice. Be born twice [on Earth and born again in Christ] and die once!"

> Everyone who calls on the name of the LORD [to place their trust in Jesus Christ] will be saved. Romans 10:13

Summary of Chapter Six

- The Bible describes two deaths and two resurrections—the two deaths represent two separations from God.
- Man, like God, his creator, has a triune nature—man's nature is body, soul, and spirit.
- Believers who have trusted Christ for salvation will be resurrected at the *first resurrection* to eternal reward and joy with Christ in Heaven.
- The lost are resurrected at the *second resurrection* for judgment and condemnation to the *second death*—eternity apart from God in Hell, a fate escaped by born-again believers.

Chapter 7

"In the Middle of the Seven"

"He will confirm a covenant with many for one 'seven'. In the middle of the 'seven' he will put an end to sacrifice and offering. And on a wing [of the temple] he will set up an abomination that causes desolation, until the end that is decreed is poured out on him."

—Daniel 9:27

As discussed at length in chapter two, the term "seven" represents a period of time equivalent to:

A. Seven years of 360 days each
B. The "middle of the seven" is halfway through the seven-year period
C. A three-and-one-half year period of forty-two months of 30 days, or 1,260 days.

Some have interpreted the three-and-one-half-year ministry of Jesus the Christ (Jesus, the Anointed Minister) as fulfilling this prophecy. Those who hold to this view claim that the institution of the New Covenant put an end to the Old Covenant system of sacrifice and offering. Temple sacrifice did end with the *second* temple's destruction in the siege of Jerusalem in A.D. 70. However, the examination of related passages in other books of the Bible demonstrates that Daniel 9:27 does not refer to the Lord but to the Antichrist, the "he" of Daniel 9:27!

John wrote to believers affirming their understanding that the Antichrist would be coming (1 John 2:18). The Antichrist would arise, empowered by Satan, to dominate the world, persecute the saints, seek to destroy the Jews, and banish the name of God and His Christ from the earth. Antichrist is also called the man of lawlessness, the lawless one (2 Thessalonians 2:3–8), and the beast (Revelation 13:1–10).

Chapter twelve of Daniel opens with the focus on a distressing time such as "has not happened from the beginning of nations until then." (See Daniel 12:1.) This time of great distress was reemphasized by Jesus in Matthew 24:21 and Mark 13:19. Daniel 12 includes two specific events associated with this time of great distress, the resurrection of the multitudes who "sleep in the dust," and final judgment. According to Scripture, the *first resurrection* takes place after the time of great distress and before the thousand-year reign of Christ on Earth. The *second* resurrection and final judgment of the wicked takes place following this millennium (Revelation 20:4—15). Nineteen centuries have passed since A.D. 70 and neither of these predicted events has occurred. *How could Daniel 9:27 have been interpreted as fulfilled in A.D. 70?*

The conclusion of Daniel 12 addresses specific numbers of days associated with the abolishing of the daily sacrifice and the abomination (gross idol), causing desolation (God's people flee). This prophecy implies a *third* temple erected in Jerusalem and the temple sacrificial system reestablished in the future.

Other unfulfilled events yet to occur during the second half of Daniel's seventieth week that nullify the "preterist," or "already done," interpretation of Daniel and Revelation include the cata-strophic destruction of one-third of the earth by fire and one-third of the sea turned to blood (Revelation 8:7–9). Revelation 13 tells of an image erected to honor Antichrist, which can speak aloud, and it is prophesied that all who refuse to worship this image will be killed (Revelation 13:15).

There are several other problems with the preterist belief that most or all of biblical prophecy has been fulfilled by the year 70 A.D. After seven hundred years of gentile domination, followed by eighteen centuries of the Diaspora, the nation of Israel was rebirthed in a single day (May 14, 1948). The Hebrew language has been revived as the national tongue, and the fate of Jerusalem is the focus of international concern. These events are literal fulfillments of Isaiah 66:8, Ezekiel 37:1–14, and Zechariah 12:2.

The interpretation that all the events prophesied by Daniel were fulfilled in 70 A.D. seems to be in error. Daniel 9:27 is yet to be fulfilled.

Why was this A.D. 70 *preterist* doctrine formed? The answer may lie in the near fulfillment of Daniel's events in archetype.

To a degree, many of the prophesied events of the final Great Tribulation period *have* been fulfilled in "type and shadow" (looks like the fulfillment but only a partial fulfillment or a picture of the final fulfillment). During the reign of Antiochus IV Epiphanes, there was great persecution; the temple in Jerusalem was defiled and an image erected. Again, during the time of the Roman siege of Jerusalem by General Titus, there was great persecution and the temple and the city were destroyed. These events only fore-shadow the unparalleled great distress to occur at the end of this age. There is literal fulfillment of prophecy still to come concern-ing the last world empire and the evil Antichrist king who will exalt and magnify himself (Daniel 11:36).

To gain deeper insight into the composition and nature of the worldwide empire due before Christ's reign, it is helpful to study former empires, which have ruled many nations, and as recorded in the Bible. The books of Daniel and Revelation are replete with visions of beasts (powerful political and military empires). These powerful and ferocious beasts reflect the character and nature of certain nations that have dominated world history. They acceded to power and maintained rule by force and oppression. Surely, many of the kings of these empires were empowered by the same domineering spirit!

Why is this final world power a "red" empire?

> Then another sign appeared in heaven: an enormous red dragon with seven heads and ten horns and seven crowns on His heads.
> Revelation 12:3

Revelation 12:9 states that the "great dragon who was hurled down is that ancient serpent" called the devil or Satan. The dragon is red in color. Scarlet or crimson represents sin (confer with Isaiah 1:18 for one example). Satan (Lucifer), a liar and thief, was created full of wisdom and beauty (Ezekiel 28:12) and was known as the morning star (Lucifer means "light bearer").

Lucifer, as a beautiful cherub, led the worship of God in the highest heaven. In his pride and jealousy, he coveted worship for himself and led one-third of the angels in revolt against God (Revelation 12:4). The devil was cast down as a bolt of lightning looks when cast to the earth (Luke 10:18). Biblical names often reflect the character of the individual. Lucifer is now known therefore as "Satan," which means, "adversary." His fallen angels are called demons or devils. Satan, the chief of the demons, is known also as the Devil. The seven heads of his enormous red dragon represent seven kings or world leaders.

"They [the seven heads] are also seven kings. Five have fallen, one is, the other has not yet come; but when he does come he must remain for a little while." Revelation 17:10

What does Satan desire? Why the universal conflict with God? Satan desires worship, an honor merited by God alone, as in the first two commandments in Exodus 20. Satan tempted Jesus in the wilderness to worship him as a god. He was enabled to offer Jesus all the authority and splendor of the kingdoms of the world during the temptation (Matthew 4:8–9; Luke 4:5–7) because they were Satan's to give since man forfeited dominion over the earth with the fall of Eden. Satan is the crowned prince of this world (John 12:31).

As for you, you were dead in your transgressions and sins, in which you used to live when you followed the way of this world and of the ruler of the kingdom of the air, the spirit who is now at work in those who are disobedient. Ephesians 2:1–2

Satan is the spirit who is at work in those who are separated from God by sin. Satan works through earthly kings and rulers to accomplish his goals. There are human and demonic agencies at work in world governments. The Bible offers two illustrations of this principle in the prophesied judgments against the king of Babylon (Isaiah 14:12–20) and the king of Tyre (Ezekiel 28:1–19). These passages of Scripture describe men who bear characteristics of Satan and also refer directly to Satan himself.

At the time of the writing of the book of Revelation, Israel had suffered captivity and domination by five empires over time, each of which had fallen from positions of leadership. Each kingdom had ruled over many nations and enslaved many peoples at the height of its power. These former world powers in order of appearance on the world scene: Egypt; Assyria; Babylon; Medo-Persia; Greece; and Rome. The one head of the beast still in power at the time of John's exile to Patmos (See Revelation 1:9) was the ruler of the last empire, Rome. The head or king yet to come and reign for a brief time will be ruler over the final world empire, the coming man of sin, the Antichrist.

The dragon bears seven crowns on his heads. The crowns signify that each world ruler had power in past times and authority to rule as given by Satan under God's sovereign plan. God is the ultimate ruler over Satan and all creation. Satan has a legal right, however, limited by God's ordained boundaries, to exercise demonic influence over sinful man.

When we submit to God and resist the devil in the authority of Jesus Christ, therefore, Satan must flee (James 4:7), but those who seek power, wealth, and self-glorification instead serve the devil.

What is the difference between the dragon with seven horns and Revelation's ten-horned dragon? The enormous red dragon had *ten*, not seven, horns. To understand the significance of the ten horns, Daniel's "ten *toes*" may shed scriptural light on the ten *horns* of Revelation.

According to Daniel 1:1, Nebuchadnezzer, king of Babylon, came to Jerusalem during the reign of Jehoiakim, king of Judah, and laid siege to the city (605 B.C.). After a long occupation, in 586 B.C., the Babylonians destroyed Jerusalem and the temple. During the course of the Babylonian assault, there were three deportations of exiles from Judah to Babylonia. Daniel was among the first of the Judeans taken captive. Daniel was groomed for service in the Babylonian court along with three good chums, Hananiah (Shadrach), Mishael (Meshach), and Azariah (Abednego).

Daniel and friends demonstrated righteous character and obedience to God by a refusal to become defiled by eating or drinking the rich diet and wine of the royal court. Pagan ritual included offering the first portions of the royal food and drink to idols.

Many of the meats came from "unclean" animals forbidden the Jewish people by God's command. Even acceptable animal meat from ceremonially clean animals would be defiled since the meat would not be drained of blood as Scripture prescribes. (See Leviticus 17:11.) God blessed Daniel's faithfulness and granted him superb wisdom and the ability to interpret God-given visions and dreams (Daniel 1:17).

In the second year of Nebuchadnezzer's reign, the king was deeply troubled and had difficulty in sleeping due to a greatly disturbing dream. (See Daniel 2:1.) No court magician or astrologer could tell the king his dream by use of their occult arts. Furious at their inability to help, the king ordered the execution of all the "wise men" of Babylon, which would have condemned Daniel and his three friends as court officials as well. The four men sought God in prayer, pleading for mercy in regard to a revealing of the king's dream. During the night, the mystery was revealed to Daniel in a vision (Daniel 2:19). This astounding dream and prophecy highlights the rise and fall of past and present world empires.

What "dragon empires" did Nebuchadnezzar's dream reveal through Daniel? Nebuchadnezzer once dreamt of an enormous, dazzling statue of a man. The statue's head was made of purest gold, its chest and arms of silver, its belly and thighs of bronze, its legs of iron, and its feet and toes partly of iron and partly of crumbling clay. As the king watched, a quarried rock, not cut away by human hands, smashed the statue to dust. A wind blew the dust away without leaving a trace of the statue, and then the rock that struck and destroyed the statue grew to a mountain filling the whole earth. Daniel interpreted this dream as a prophetic picture representing Babylon and the subsequent empires to follow in world rule until the return of Christ. The rock "cut out without human hands" is Christ Himself, who will obliterate wicked rulers and their oppressive empires. When the final empire is vanquished,

Christ will set up His glorious, literal millennial kingdom of 1,000 years' rule.

The gold head of Nebuchadnezzer's dream clearly represented Babylon; the silver chest and arms, the Medo-Persian empire; the bronze belly and thighs, Greek power; the iron legs, ancient Rome; and the feet and toes mixed of iron and clay, the final world empire. The ten mixed toes correspond to the ten horns of the enormous red dragon of Revelation. A confederation or alliance of ten nation-states or world regions will comprise a power base for Antichrist.

Daniel himself received a number of dreams and visions (dreamt during the reign of Belshazzar, a successor to the throne of Nebuchadnezzer) concerning the then-world empires to come. Daniel said:

"In my vision at night I looked, and there before me were the four winds of heaven churning up the great sea. Four great beasts, each different from the others, came out of the sea." Daniel 7:2

Compare Daniel's statement with Isaiah, who said: "But the wicked are like the tossing sea, which cannot rest, whose waves cast up mire and mud" (Isaiah 57:20).

The churning sea of Isaiah symbolizes wicked humanity! The beasts of Scripture are ceremonially unclean animals, representative of gentile nations (Acts 10:9–23). Each beast or nation rises out of the wicked sea of humanity—and to power.

Earthly beasts dominate and devour according to their speed, sizes, and strength. In a similar vein, at times in world history, certain nations have risen to power by devouring and trampling down their adversaries. Each beast of Daniel's vision parallels a segment of the statue of Nebuchadnezzer's dream. The first beast like a lion with eagle's wings pictured Babylon. The second beast, looking like a bear, represented Medo-Persia.

The third beast that looked like a leopard with four wings and four heads represented the empire ruled by Alexander the Great.

After his death, his generals divided Alexander's massive domain into four kingdoms (the four heads of the leopard beast).

- Ptolemy I ruled over Egypt and North Africa
- Seleusus gained "Syria" and Mesopotamia
- Lysimachus obtained Thrace and Asia Minor
- Cassander ruled over Alexander's native Macedonia

The fourth beast represented the Roman Empire and was a terrifying, frightening, and powerful beast with teeth of iron and ten horns. Rome certainly fit this "teeth of iron" description—countless thousands were pierced with nails of iron as they were crucified. Many others were thrown to lions or wild dogs, torn apart for entertainment in the Roman circus.

> "He [God's angel] gave me this explanation: 'The fourth beast is a fourth kingdom that will appear on earth. It will be different from all the other kingdoms and will devour the whole earth, trampling it down and crushing it. The ten horns are ten kings who will come from this kingdom. After them another king will arise, different from the earlier ones; he will subdue three kings.'" Daniel 7:23–24

> "The ten horns you saw are ten kings who have not yet received a kingdom, but who for one hour will receive authority as kings along with the beast. They have one purpose and will give their power and authority to the beast." Revelation 17:12–13

The world empire to come will be comprised of a ten nation confederacy or ten region alliance whose rulers (the ten kings) will lend their support to an eleventh leader—Antichrist.

The Antichrist will arise during Daniel's seventieth week to rule over the final empire, empowered by the alliance of ten rulers.

The three and one-half-year reign of terror by the Antichrist will be the subject of our next chapter.

Summary of Chapter Seven

- The Antichrist will abolish worship sacrifices at the coming third temple of Jerusalem.
- Daniel 9:27 teaches that 1,260 days (three and one-half biblical years) into the tribulation will be the day of Antichrist's temple blasphemy and persecution.
- Revelation and Daniel cross-reference each other and help us interpret both together; they reveal a devilish Antichrist who will rule over a ten-nation confederacy of nation-states.
- The final empire before Christ's return to Earth is pictured in the major world powers prophesied in Nebuchadnezzar's dream of a great statue and Daniel's vision of beastly creatures.
- Daniel and Revelation connote a literal three and one-half-year reign of Antichrist, explored in the next chapter.

Chapter 8

The Saints Will Be Handed to Him

"He [Antichrist] will speak against the Most High and oppress His saints and try to change the set times and the laws. The saints will be handed over to him for a time, times and half a time."

—Daniel 7:25

As discussed in chapter seven, Daniel's night vision of four beasts was interpreted as symbolizing four kingdoms to rise from the earth (Daniel 7:17). The fourth and most terrifying beast, with iron teeth and bronze claws, had ten horns on its head, corresponding to the ten horns of the scarlet beast of Revelation 17. An eleventh horn arose on this horrible beast, more imposing than the others. The imposing horn that arises after the ten, that is, in the coming future, is Antichrist. Antichrist will speak horrible blasphemies against God:

"The king will do as he pleases. He will exalt and magnify himself above every god and will say unheard of things against the God of gods." Daniel 11:36

He will attempt to abrogate the laws of God given to Moses at Mt. Sinai:

> "You shall have no other gods before me. You shall not make for yourself an idol in the form of anything in the heaven above or on the earth beneath or in the waters below . . . You shall not misuse the name of the LORD your God, for the LORD will not hold anyone guiltless who misuses His name." Exodus 20:4–7

The Antichrist is supremely arrogant and boastful. He extols and magnifies himself. In self-exaltation and rebellion against God, he blasphemes the name of the LORD. The Antichrist is guilty of intentional and presumptuous sin. It is his intention to take the name of the LORD in vain to flagrantly violate the third commandment of Exodus 20. The second commandment forbade the making of or bowing to idols for the Israelites, but an image of Antichrist will be erected in his honor! Under penalty of death for refusing homage to his image, people will be forced to prostrate before the idol of Antichrist. (See Revelation 13:15.) Multitudes will be corrupted by flattery, and Antichrist will greatly honor those who acknowledge him by making them rulers (Daniel 11:32; 39). Through Satan, who covets worship for himself, Antichrist will turn the hearts of the masses in apostasy from the one true God—and to transgress the greatest of the commandments, to love God above all. (See Mark 12:29.)

> But mark this: There will be terrible times in the last days. People will be lovers of themselves; lovers of money, boastful, proud, abusive, disobedient to parents, ungrateful, unholy, without love, unforgiving, slanderous, without self-control, brutal, not lovers of the good, treacherous, rash, conceited, lovers of pleasure rather than lovers of God. 2 Timothy 3:1–4

With the secularization of modern society, the absolutes of God's moral law have been replaced with humanistic precepts of situation ethics. Sins are renamed to "addictions" and have become politically correct and fashionable. The murder of children in the womb is a "reproductive right." Sexual perversions are sexual "lifestyles." Rates of infidelity, divorce, alcoholism and drug addiction, child abuse, and gambling are soaring. Even plagues of sexually transmitted diseases, including incurable and deadly epidemics, have not stemmed the tide of debauchery. The focus is upon self-gratification without regard to consequence or responsibility.

Following the lead of a decrepit society, undoubtedly much like our own, Antichrist will usher in a "new age" as demonic activity flourishes. The detestable ways of the nations of Canaan (Deuteronomy 18:9–12) caused God's anger to burn against their sin. Will it be different for this present generation, which embraces detestable Canaanite practices—consulting psychics, mediums, astrologers, and other practitioners of the occult arts, those who promise relief from trouble and judgment apart from God's help?

In describing the generation of Noah's day, Scripture states man's extreme wickedness, perverseness, and violence:

> The LORD saw how great man's wickedness on the earth had become, and that every inclination of the thoughts of His heart was only evil all the time. Genesis 6:5

Jesus foretold that before His triumphant return the world would be as it was in Noah's day. Those who hold to the pre-tribulation view of the coming rapture cite Enoch's rapture to be with God *before* the worldwide flood. (See Genesis 5:24.). Since Enoch (a human type of Christians alive at Christ's coming) walked with God and since the Noahic flood foreshadows final judgment, as in 2 Peter 3:6–7, a pre-tribulation rapture is concluded. There is a subtle fallacy in this understanding—Enoch was taken sixty-nine years before Noah's birth. Enoch's life was never part of the days of Noah!

Before the rapture, the saints must be purified in refining fires of persecution. "If anyone is to go into captivity, into captivity he will go. If anyone is to be killed with the sword, with the sword he will be killed. This calls for patient endurance and faithfulness on the part of the saints" (Revelation 13:10)

The Lord, in His supreme wisdom and mercy, will allow the cup of man's iniquity to reach its fill before pouring out the full measure of His wrath. To purify His bride (Revelation 19:7–8) and turn the hearts of the people of the nation of Israel back to the one they have pierced (Zechariah 12:10), God will allow Antichrist to oppress and persecute the saints for some time, specifically, "a time [one year], times [two years] and half a time [one-half year]." This expression totals three and one-half years and is equivalent to 1,260 days. *"For the sake of the elect,"* this time of horrible trouble will be "cut short" by the rapture (Matthew 24:22). Jesus Himself learned obedience from suffering and was perfected by enduring trials and the cross (Hebrews 5:8–9).

"All men will hate you because of me, but he who stands firm to the end [remains faithful despite persecution of the tribulation period due to their assurance in Christ] will be saved." Matthew 10:22

"Remember the words I spoke to you: 'No servant is greater than His master.' If they persecuted me, they will persecute you also." John 15:20a

Therefore put on the full armor of God, so that when the day of evil comes, you may be able to stand your ground, and after you have done everything, to stand. Ephesians 6:13

Christians are to anticipate persecution and trials. When tribulation comes, we are to stand firm in the faith. The saints must pray and be in the Word daily to stand effectively in evil times. We must stand firm and not compromise or renounce the faith. Surely the prophesied time of great distress and evil is soon at hand. Antichrist, the man of perdition (or literally, the "son of Hell") will vent fury against the righteous. Many will be imprisoned, others martyred. Blessed are those who are persecuted for righteousness sake, however. Jesus proclaimed that those suffering persecution should rejoice due to their great heavenly reward (Matthew 5:12). Christians have been forewarned to not be in darkness that evil times should surprise us like a thief entering our homes unexpectedly. (See 1 Thessalonians 5:4.)

Scripture relating to the end of this age does not proclaim escape from the tribulation to come but rather encouragement to patiently endure. We are to be strengthened in our faith (should we live to see Revelation's events unfold) that the Bible is perfect and true. Only omniscient God can foretell and proclaim the future with 100% precision. "Be strong in the Lord and in the power of His might," Ephesians 6:10 tells us. Sadly, many unbelievers will reject God's revelation and will be unprepared mentally and spiritually for times of trouble ahead.

> First of all, you must understand that in the last days scoffers will come, scoffing and following their own evil desires. They will say, "Where is this 'coming' he promised?" 2 Peter 3:3–4a

Pre-tribulation teaching is immensely popular in the Western evangelical church. If events unfold soon without a change in doctrine to pre-wrath rapture, many could face imprisonment and death for their faith, bewildered as to why they have not been raptured but are being persecuted! Their confusion could potentially cause their captors to jeer at the "coming" of Christ. Unlike the first century Church that rejoiced because they were worthy of suffering disgrace for Christ and grew in vast numbers (Acts 5:41), unbelievers will turn, scoffing, from the faith (Matthew 24:10).

> Consider it pure joy, my brothers, whenever you face trials of many kinds, because you know that the testing of your faith develops perseverance. Perseverance must finish its work so that you may be mature and complete, not lacking anything. James 1:2–4

When Jesus returns for His bride, His Church will be mature and complete, having endured through the time of great distress. Indeed, the blood of the righteous has been spilled over the centuries so often; in Old Testament times, from Abel to Zechariah (Matthew 23:35), yet the Church has prevailed.

> Others were tortured and refused to be released, so that they may gain a better resurrection. Some faced jeers and flogging, while still others were chained and put in prison. They were stoned, they were sawed in two; they were put to death by the sword. They went about in sheepskins and goatskins, destitute, persecuted and mistreated—the world was not worthy of them . . . Hebrews 11:35–38

Not only were Old Testament prophets persecuted but also the first century Church. Tradition says that John the Apostle was exiled and that nine of ten other of Jesus' closest disciples were martyred for their faith.

> Let us fix our eyes on Jesus, the author and perfecter of our faith, who for the joy set before him endured the cross, scorning its shame, and sat down at the right hand of the throne of God. Hebrews 12:2

We must not lose heart or grow weary in doing good works. We must have the mind of Christ Jesus who looked past the shame and suffering of the cross to the joy and reward of doing the will of the Father. We must maintain an eternal perspective. Paul, who was beaten with rods, flogged, and stoned for his faith said: "I consider that our present sufferings are not worth comparing with the glory that will be revealed in us" (Romans 8:18).

Although for a short time it will seem as if evil prevails during the horrible trials of the tribulation period, the victory is firm for each believer, in the hands of Christ:

> "They overcame him by the blood of the Lamb and by the word of their testimony; they did not love their lives so much as to shrink from death." Revelation 12:11

Summary of Chapter Eight

- Antichrist will staunchly blaspheme God's righteous commandments by declaring himself honor and with divine attributes.
- If Christians will indeed experience the horrors of the tribulation period, then pre-tribulation teachings are in danger of frustrating and demoralizing Christ's Church.
- Regardless, biblical Christians will overcome the tribulation period—Christ guarantees salvation and a viable witness to those who trust in Him: "Those who are wise will instruct many, though for a time they will fall by the sword or be burned or captured or plundered" (Daniel 11:33).
- The tribulation's second half will be abbreviated by its days being "cut short," nullifying the possibility of the date of Christ's return being calculated precisely—beware false prophets who would dare to date the return of Jesus Christ!

. . . .

Chapter 9

"The Dragon Gave the Beast . . ."

And I saw a beast coming out of the sea. He had ten horns and seven heads, with ten crowns on His horns, and on each head a blasphemous name. The beast I saw resembled a leopard, but had feet like those of a bear and a mouth like that of a lion. The dragon gave the beast His power and His throne and great authority. One of the heads of the beast seemed to have a fatal wound, but the fatal wound had been healed. The whole world was astonished and followed the beast.

—Revelation 13:1–3

The beast of Revelation 13 emerges from "the sea" with seven heads and ten crowned horns. Contrast this description with the scarlet beast of Revelation 12 appearing in Heaven, also with seven heads and *ten horns but only seven crowns on its heads.*

Crowns symbolize power and authority. The dragon of Revelation 12, Satan, led rebellion in Heaven and was cast to Earth, taking a third of God's angels with him in conspiracy (Revelation 12:4). The *seven* crowns on its *heads* represent satanic power and authority, empowering the rulers of empires. In the ancient world, rulers of Egypt, Assyria, Babylon, Medo-Persia, Greece, and Rome were empowered by their occult, polytheistic mystery religions. Worshippers of themselves or idols, they were indeed offering the children of their kingdoms as demonic sacrifices (Psalm 106:36–37). In the future, Antichrist will also rule with power and authority from Satan. He will be the last and most heinous emperor of all! The scarlet beast with seven horns symbolizes governmental agencies employed by Satan throughout world history until the end of this age.

The ten-crowned beast is somewhat different in nature, in composition. The beast with *ten* crowns of Revelation 13 is not a sign in Heaven but emerges out of "the sea," the teeming sea of wicked humanity as mentioned in chapter seven. This beast also has seven heads and ten horns, but its crowns are on his *horns*, not its heads. Power and authority, given to the horns, symbolize ten human kings who relinquish their immense power and authority to the Antichrist (Revelation 17:13). On each *head* is written a blasphemous name.

What is a "blasphemy"? Blasphemy can be irreverent speech concerning God or *speech attributing God's divine attributes to sinful man.* The Jews wanted to stone Jesus because they understood His claim to divinity, and they believed he was merely a man. (See John 10:31–33.) The Lord Jesus Christ was, of course, God Himself and therefore innocent of any charge of blasphemy. Colossians 2:9 states, "For in Christ all the fullness of the Deity lives in bodily form . . ." Blasphemous names on each of the ten heads of Revelation 17 might be pretentious titles falsely proclaiming the kings as gods or the names of the kings as names worshipped as gods.

Countless pagan rulers have erected images of themselves for worship. Many also have claimed to be a god in human form. For one example, the nation of Israel was enslaved for 400 years in Egypt, first of the biblical world empires under discussion. Pharaoh, title of the Egyptian kings, was identified with the Sun gods. The chief Egyptian god, "Amon-Re," was believed embodied in

Pharaoh's human person. The Egyptians believed Pharaoh to be omnipotent and omniscient—Egypt's mightiest god.

The Northern Kingdom of ten of the tribes of Israel was literally exported into captivity by the second world empire under discussion, Assyria. "Tiglath-Pileser" was the title of three different kings of Assyria. In the Assyrians' language, Tiglath-Pileser would be instead "Tukulti-apal-Esarra" or "my help is the first born of the Esharra Temple" (the god Assur). Tiglath-Pileser II, who brought Israel into captivity, set up bas-reliefs (sculptures) with his divine, royal image in numerous conquered cities. In other words, the Assyrians, like the Egyptians, deified their leaders.

The third world empire to emerge was Babylon. King Nebuchadnezzer laid Jerusalem waste and stole many captives from the Southern Kingdom of Judah and Benjamin. Daniel recounts that while walking on the roof of the magnificent royal palace of Babylon, perhaps adoring the ancient wonder of the hanging gardens, Nebuchadnezaar proclaimed:

> "Is not this the great Babylon I have built as the royal residence of my mighty power and for the glory of my majesty?" Daniel 4:30

For his haughtiness (God had already humbled and spoken to Nebuchadnezzar through Daniel), Nebuchadnezzer was inflicted immediately with what is called *boanthropy*. Made to live as a wild animal, Nebuchadnezzar's hair grew long and unkempt, and his nails grew into veritable claws. (Secular history seems to confirm that Nebuchadnezzar lived in the royal gardens and his viceroy ruled in his stead.) He was humbled until he came to acknowledge that God alone is sovereign over the kingdoms of men (Daniel 4:32). King Belshazzar, a successor and descendant of King Nebuchadnezzer, despite knowing God's sovereignty over the kingdoms of men (Daniel 5:21), defied God and desecrated the sacred vessels of the temple of Jerusalem. Like Antichrist who is coming, Belshazzar sinned with blasphemy not in ignorance but intentionally with pride and arrogance. Belshazzar praised idols and dishonored God during an orgy of revelry and blasphemy. The third empire also had deified its leaders.

The fourth empire to emerge was the Medo-Persian Empire. Darius the Mede took over the Babylonian Empire the very night Daniel interpreted the "writing on the wall" (Daniel 5:22–28). Again, we would expect the fourth empire as a type of Antichrist's confederation to sin by blaspheming God. In celebration of the Persian New Year, groups of officials from twenty satrapies, or kingdom divisions, marched through Persepolis, ceremonial capital of Persia. Paying homage to Darius, they dared to call him "king of kings."

Darius' own people and the conquered Greeks and other subjugated peoples later esteemed another biblical ruler of the Medo-Persians, Cyrus II. Cyrus culled favor from the peoples he conquered by supporting their local customs and sacrificing to their local gods and the Persian gods. Although the Lord designated Cyrus by name through his prophet and bestowed honor on him (see Isaiah 45:4–5), Cyrus paid homage to Marduk and seems to have little acknowledged the God of Israel.

Alexander the Great established the fifth of the world empires. Following great accomplishments in battle, Alexander became convinced of his own divinity. He was pleased to be compared to Dionysus, Greek god of wine and ecstasy. Likewise, the sixth of the historic empires was Rome, where the title of Caesar was taken by or given to each Roman emperor following Julius Caesar's example. Caesar is the imperial title of New Testament record. Those who held that Christ and not Caesar is Lord were persecuted, humiliated, and often martyred for faith. Failure to worship Caesar or bow to his image was viewed as high treason against the Roman State.

The seventh empire or beast's head is the coming kingdom of Antichrist and little different in its blasphemy than the previous six world rulers under study. The Antichrist will blaspheme by speaking evil of God (Daniel 11:36). He will desecrate the third temple with an image of himself (Revelation 13:15) and claim divinity (Daniel 11:37). Antichrist, as was said of King Ahab of Israel in his day, will exceed in evil than any before him (1 Kings 16:30).

Who is this blasphemer, Antichrist, the seventh head of the beast and ruler of the seventh coming empire? The name of the beast is yet to be revealed, but we can examine the number of the Antichrist.

> He also forced everyone, small and great, rich and poor, free and slave, to receive a mark on His right hand or on His forehead, so that no one could buy or sell unless he had the mark, which is the name of the beast or the number of His name. This calls for wisdom. If anyone has insight, let him calculate the number of the beast, for it is man's number. His number is 666. Revelation 13:16–18

[Author's note: During Antichrist's reign, a second leader will perform miraculous signs (see Revelation 13:13). He will have authority to force the inhabitants of the earth to worship Antichrist and receive the beast's mark. This evil enforcer is commonly known as the False Prophet (the subject of our next chapter.) People may submit to receiving Antichrist's mark or face prospects of imprisonment and death (Revelation 13:10).]

To determine the calculated number of Antichrist's name, one must calculate the number of the Revelation 13 beast. In other words, we might assign numerical value to each letter of Antichrist's name and then obtain a sum of the numbers, totaling 666.

It would not be wise to add the number using Antichrist's name in the English language. In the English speaking world, we use a Roman letter system (our alphabet), and we have a separate system for cardinal, or Arabic, numerals. The three biblical alphabets of Hebrew, Greek, and Aramaic do not add a separate system of symbols representing numbers. Rather, the letters of these languages have numerical values assigned to them, and letters can do double duty.

For example, the Greek alphabet assigns both the number one (1) and the letter A to its *Alpha*; *Beta* indicates either B or 2; *Gamma* can mean C or 3; and so on. Likewise, in Hebrew the letters *Aleph*, *Beth*, and *Gimel* may be used for A, B, and C or 1, 2, and 3, respectively. (See the chart below.) We can look at the numerical value of *Jesus* in the Greek:

Jesus: "IHSOYS":

I	"Iota"	10
H	"Eta"	8
S	"Sigma"	200
O	"Omicron"	70
Y	"Upsilon"	400
S	"Sigma"	200

Total: *888*

"Alpha"	1	a	A
"Beta"	2	b	B
"Gamma"	3	g	G
"Delta"	4	s	D
"Epsilon"	5	e	E
"Zeta"	7	z	Z
"Eta"	8	h	H

"Theta"	9	q	Q
"Iota"	10	i	I
"Kappa"	20	k	K
"Lambda"	30	l	L
"Mu"	40	m	M
"Nu"	50	n	N
"Xi"	60	x	X
"Omicron"	70	o	O
"Pi"	80	p	P
"Rho"	100	r	R
"Sigma"	200	s, V	S
"Tau"	300	t	T
"Upsilon"	400	u	U
"Phi"	500	f	F
"Chi"	600	c	C
"Psi"	700	y	Y
"Omega"	800	w	W

So, why use "666" as the number to represent Antichrist?

let him (who is endowed with God's wisdom) calculate the number of the beast, for it is man's number. His number is 666. Revelation 13:18b

The number 666 is of course fundamentally composed of sixes:

So God created man in His own image, in the image of God he created him; male and female he created them . . . And there was evening, and there was morning—the sixth day. Genesis 1:27; 31b

Man was created in God's image on day six of the creation week. Man's number is six. By the seventh day, God finished His creation work and rested from His work (Genesis 2:2). Day six of the creation week focuses on humanity, while day seven focuses upon God and the completion of His handiwork.

God is perfect and complete in every way. Men fall short of God's perfection. The number seven, in contrast to the earthly six, is associated with heavenly perfection and completeness. The number seven appears fifty-two times in the book of Revelation. The golden lampstand that stood in the Holy Place, where the priests ministered in the tabernacle and in the temple, had seven lamps (see Exodus 25:31–40), which represented the "seven spirits" (some Bible translations read instead "sevenfold" spirit) of God.

> Then I saw a Lamb looking as if it had been slain, standing in the center of the throne, encircled by the four living creatures and the elders. He had seven horns and seven eyes which are the seven spirits of God sent out into all the earth. Revelation 5:6

Examining Antichrist's name after he is revealed to man, we may calculate his name's "gematric equivalent" (the re-working of biblical letters to their equivalent numerical values) to be 666; therefore, as the number seven represents heavenly perfection and completeness, the number six represents sinful man who is imperfect and incomplete. The number 666 may remind us that man falls short three ways—in body, soul, and spirit—of God's glorious nature. Antichrist exemplifies this complete "triple six" sinfulness of mankind. He is totally corrupt and debased, carnally-minded, blasphemous, and lives in spiritual darkness. He is the bondservant of Satan, numbered 666.

One definition of the term "Antichrist" means "against Christ" or "false (replacement of) Christ." The Antichrist will stand against all righteousness and truth. He also will be a satanic liar and deceiver.

And no wonder, for Satan himself masquerades as an angel of light. It is not surprising, then, if His servants masquerade as servants of righteousness. Their end will be what their actions deserve. 2 Corinthians 11:14–15

Jesus answered: "Watch out that no one deceive you. For many will come in my name, claiming 'I am the Christ,' and will deceive many." Matthew 24:4

Then I heard one of the four living creatures say in a voice like thunder, "Come!" I looked, and there before me was a white horse! Its rider held a bow, and he was given a crown, and he rode out as a conqueror bent on conquest. Revelation 6:1–2

There is a scroll on which are recorded events of the end of this age. It is sealed by seven seals (Revelation 5:1). When the first seal opens, it will reveal a rider on a white horse. A horse is the mount of a king when he rides to wage war (white is the color symbolizing purity and truth). This rider is carrying a bow but no arrow. He *seems to be* a man of peace. He is wearing a crown, which symbolizes kingly authority and power. This deceiver is disguised, then, as an angel of light and a man of peace. In actuality, he is bent on conquest—he's the Antichrist!

Jesus, the true Messiah, also rides a white horse in Revelation but with a sharp sword coming from His mouth to strike the nations for their wickedness (Revelation 19:15). The masses do not rely on the Word of God to reveal truth. The Holy Spirit does not live within them to bear very clear witness to absolute truth. Satan, who has blinded the minds of unbelievers (see 2 Corinthians 4:4), will deceive millions with counterfeit miracle signs.

The coming of the lawless one will be in accordance with the work of Satan displayed in all kinds of counterfeit miracles, signs and wonders. 2 Thessalonians 2:9

One such sign commonly misunderstood by the Church is the counterfeit resurrection sign. Read the following verse carefully, for most have understood Antichrist to literally rise from the dead:

> One of the heads of the beast seemed to have a fatal wound, but the fatal wound had been healed. The world was astonished and followed the beast. Revelation 13:3

To deceive the masses, Satan will arrange a feigned resurrection of Antichrist! Antichrist's seemingly fatal wound will be "healed," and the astonished populace of the world will follow the beast. The wound is a head wound, and the body of the Antichrist is not injured. Satan cannot give life (!), but he can possess the body of Antichrist and fake a resurrection or deceive unbelievers in some other way.

> As soon as Judas took the bread, Satan entered into him. John 13:27

Just as Satan entered Judas Iscariot, he will enter the Antichrist.

> "The beast, which you saw, once was, now is not, and will come up out of the Abyss and go to His destruction . . ." Revelation 17: 8a

Satan will be bound for 1,000 years, locked into the Abyss (Revelation 20:1–2). After his release, he will deceive the nations and lead a vast army against God's people. Fire will rain from Heaven and destroy Satan's army, and the devil will be tossed into Hell (Revelation 20:10). "The beast" is one term for the Antichrist. But it is the devil himself that comes from the abyss to his final destruction and inhabits the body of Antichrist.

"The beast who once was, and now is not, is an eighth king. He belongs to the seven and is going to His destruction." Revelation 17:11

The beast who "once was" is Antichrist. He "now (when the events of Revelation 17 unfold) is not," means simply that he "died." The seven horns are the heads of empires or kings. Six kings were world empire rulers of past history. The seventh king is Antichrist who had a fatal head wound and who is also the "resurrected" eighth king! The seventh king, a man known as Antichrist, "dies," and the eighth king is Satan ruling the world in the possessed body of the fatally wounded Antichrist. The world will worship Satan and the image of Antichrist, while God's people will be persecuted and martyred for righteousness' sake.

Summary of Chapter Nine

- There are two beasts in Revelation 12 and 13—one with seven crowns on its heads and one with ten crowns on its seven horns—they are distinctly different.
- The seven-headed beast represents six world empires of history who have persecuted the Jewish people: Egypt, Assyria, Babylon, Medo-Persia, Macedonia/Greece, Rome, and the final empire of Antichrist before Christ's millennial reign on Earth.
- The blasphemous names of the ten-crowned beast represent the false god titles of the seven coming world rulers who unite under Antichrist.
- The famous "666" of Antichrist probably represents the gematric equivalent of Antichrist's name in the Hebrew, Greek, and Aramaic languages. English-language derived gematria "revelations" should be more than carefully scrutinized!

- "666" represents utter sinfulness and blasphemous imperfection. Antichrist will be utterly corrupt, utterly blasphemous.
- Antichrist feigns the person and much of the work of Christ, performing miracles as does his false prophet. Antichrist feigns a "resurrection" like Christ's true bodily resurrection, using satanic power. Martyrdom is the typical fate destined for those who resist the Antichrist.

Chapter 10

"Like a Lamb . . . But He Spoke Like a Dragon"

Then I saw another beast, coming out of the earth. He had two horns like a lamb, but he spoke like a dragon.

—Revelation 13:11

The book of Revelation records that the Apostle John was shown three different beasts in a vision. Each beast emerged from a different location. The first beast John saw was an enormous red dragon, which appeared as a sign in Heaven (Revelation 12:3).

What is the significance of the scarlet beast's appearance in Heaven? Heaven's location is invisible to man and exists within the spirit realm. The description of the first beast reveals spiritual insight into the true nature (Satan-empowered) of governments whose rulers are blasphemous men. This beast had seven heads and ten horns crowned with seven crowns. This beast is a picture of seven world empires spiritually empowered by Satan. Six heads were emperors/empires of the ancient world. The seventh empire is to be ruled by the Antichrist. He will rule over a wicked and perverse generation and persecute God's saints until the sounding of the "seventh trumpet."

What was John's second beast? The second beast John saw came out of "the sea." This beast resembled a leopard but had feet like those of a bear and a mouth like a lion's (Revelation 13:2). According to the corresponding prophecies of Daniel 7, which match secular and archaeological records of the style of empires, the leopard symbolized the empire of the Greeks, the bear depicted the Medo-Persian dynasty, and lions symbolized Babylon.

Daniel also envisioned a fourth and quite terrifying beast. This beast was a picture of the iron power and ferocity of the Roman Empire. The mass of Rome's empire encompassed the occupied territories of the Greeks, Medes, and Babylon, thus the unusual beast with facets like a leopard, a bear, and a lion that John saw!

The final world empire to come will emerge from "the sea" of wicked humanity. It will be the most inhumane and ravenous in history. The term "beast" is quite an apt description and title for its vicious ruler, Antichrist. The world kingdom of the Antichrist will extend to the boundaries of ancient Rome—Britain in the far west; the Euphrates river in the east; the Arabian and Sahara desert peninsulas on the south; the Rhine, the Danube, and the Black Sea on the north.

Studying biblical prophecy as geography, it is important to note that Antichrist's empire's northern border does not extend to the territory of modern day Russia. "Directions" in the Bible always refer to points toward or away from the land of Israel. Russia's territory will not be controlled by Antichrist during the last days.

Is modern Russia mentioned in the prophecies of the Bible? The biblical "land of the far north" is modern day Russia. The prophet Ezekiel spoke of a mighty army from the far north, along with many nations, that will descend on and attack Israel (Ezekiel 38:14–15). The leader of this horde is "Gog" of the land of "Magog," chief prince of Meshech and Tubal (Ezekiel 38:2–3). Some scholars identify Meshech as Moscow and Tubal as Tobolsk in Russia. Gog rules the land of Magog, which means, "head." The Hebrew word for head is "*rosh*." The NIV's textual note gives the alternate translation for "Gog" as meaning, "prince of Rosh."

The domain of Antichrist will include neither Russia nor lands east of the Euphrates River. At the sounding of the trumpet by the sixth angel of Revelation, two hundred million mounted troops (not under Antichrist's authority) cross the Euphrates and slay a third of mankind (Revelation 9:14–16).

Who or what is the third beast of Revelation?

> My frame was not hidden from you when I was made in the secret place. When I was woven together in the depths of the earth. Psalm 139:15

> Then I saw another beast coming out of the earth . . . Revelation 13:11a

The third beast of Revelation does not arise out of the sea of humanity. It does not represent an empire or the Antichrist. This third beast depicts a person birthed literally of a woman's womb ("birth" is given as a euphemism in Scripture, "woven together in the depths of the earth," as man's frame is of carbon compounds from the dust of the earth). This person has the appearance of a lamb. A lamb is a gentle and meek creature—Christ, a lamb given for sin. This third deceiving beast has two horns as a lamb does, but he speaks like a dragon, a consuming beast.

> "Watch out for false prophets. They come to you in sheep's cloth-ing [appear to be sheep], but inwardly they are ferocious wolves." Matthew 7:15

The third beast, chief among false prophets in "ministry," is the False Prophet. There have been many false prophets just as there have been many antichrists (Matthew 24:24). The False

Prophet will be the last and most diabolical of those who speak for Satan, the great dragon. A true prophet speaks for God with authority.

Why does the Antichrist need a false prophet to accompany him? A prophet of the Lord confirmed the Word of God in his day to his listeners by miraculous signs. Moses, for example, was empowered by the Lord to do great wonders so the Israelites would believe that the God of their fathers had indeed commissioned him (Exodus 4:1–9). The False Prophet will do counterfeit signs and wonders to deceive the people in the worship of a false god and in the taking of his mark.

> If a prophet, or one who foretells by dreams, appears among you and announces to you a miraculous sign or wonder, and if the sign or wonder of which he has spoken takes place, and he says, "Let us follow other gods" [gods you have not known] and "let us worship them," you must not listen to the words of that prophet or dreamer. The LORD your God is testing you to find out whether you love him with all your heart and all your soul. Deuteronomy 13:1–3

The Church will be kept from the hour of trial testing the inhabitants of the earth (Revelation 3:10). But there will be Jewish people, not in the Church by faith in Jesus as Savior and Messiah, left on Earth to endure the terrible hour of trial. Their love of God will be tested. The False Prophet will perform tremendous signs, even causing fire to rain from Heaven (Revelation 13:13; for a fascinating comparison, confer with Exodus 9:23; Luke 9:54; Acts 2:19). To the Jewish people, the False Prophet will be a counterfeit Elijah—"preparing the way" for a false Christ.

During the festival of Passover each year, the Jewish people celebrate a tradition by pouring a cup of wine for Elijah and leaving the doors of their homes open for his prophesied visit before

Messiah's visit to Earth. Elijah was an anointed prophet of the Old Testament period of the kings. He called down fire from Heaven (1 Kings 18:36–38). Elijah did not experience death but was taken up to Heaven in a whirlwind (2 Kings 2:11). It was prophesied in the last book of the Old Testament that Elijah would return before the great and dreadful day of the LORD (Malachi 4:5).

I believe that the False Prophet, mocking Elijah's promised appearance, will begin his evil work at the Passover, which occurs midway in Daniel's seventieth week. Israel will be deceived into believing that the False Prophet is Elijah. At first, due to the False Prophet, the Jewish people will embrace Antichrist as Messiah. Soon after, Satan will feign the Antichrist's resurrection. What will happen when the False Prophet sets up an image of Antichrist to be worshipped? Many will realize the blasphemy of Antichrist's graven image—he is a false prophet according to Deuteronomy 13:1–3. Those who will not bow before his image prove to be those who love God and will realize the true Messiah who will reign over a restored Israel for 1,000 years.

The False Prophet is one-third of an evil triumvirate. In ancient Rome, a "triumvir" was any one of three key administrators who shared authority. Three destroyers will rule with cruelty over the last world empire before Christ's return and over what is geographically a revived Roman Empire at that! Spiritually, they are a most unholy trinity—counterfeits in work and authority of the Father, Son, and Holy Spirit.

Who are the "unholy trinity"? Satan covets worship and rebels against God. A deceiving spirit, Satan is called the *father* of lies (John 8:44). Like Father God in Heaven, Satan is a spirit being. (See John 4:24.) While God the Father is the author of life (*father* literally means, "life giver"), Satan takes life, a murderer through sin's destructive power. Satan is the first person of the unholy trinity.

The Antichrist is the "*son* of perdition." He is the seed of Satan through Satan's indwelling and a false Christ. He is the second person of the unholy trinity. As for the person and ministry of the Holy Spirit, who brings conviction of sin to the wicked and brings people to Christ for redemption (see John 16:8–11), the False Prophet, third member of the false trinity, by contrast persecutes the righteous as though they were evil (!) and helps force the masses to worship Antichrist.

> He (the False Prophet) was given power to give breath to the image of the first beast, (Antichrist) so that it could speak and cause all who refuse to worship the image to be killed. Revelation 13:15

What about the idolatrous image of Antichrist? Why would modern people worship such an image?

When the Lord formed Adam from the dust of the ground, He breathed into his nostrils and man became a living being (Genesis 2:7). The words for breath in both Hebrew ("*ruach*") and in Greek ("*pneuma*") may be translated as "wind" or "spirit." Jesus Christ illustrated the concept of the new spiritual birth for the born again as comparable to the strength and invisibility of the wind (John 3:6–8). When the False Prophet gives living breath to Antichrist's image, therefore, he may be deceiving through trickery, but it appears more likely that Satan will assign a living evil spirit to indwell the idol.

Why is Jerusalem key to unlocking the geographic locations of Revelation events?

> "He will confirm a covenant with many for one 'seven.' In the middle of the 'seven' he will put an end to sacrifice and offering. And on a wing of the temple he will set up an abomination that causes desolation, until the end that is decreed is poured out on him." Daniel 9:27

Scripture details that Antichrist will confirm the covenant mentioned in Daniel 9:27. Daniel's vision focused upon events concerning Jerusalem and God's own Jewish people. This agreement, or covenant, concerning Jerusalem is literally "confirmed," *indicating an already existing pact* to be ratified by the Antichrist. In the middle of the seven, or three and one-half years, after the confirmation of the covenant, temple sacrifice is abolished. On a wing of the third temple in Jerusalem, Antichrist will set up an image for worship. Jewish men and women who love God's commandments will abandon the temple because of the graven image erected there. The nation of Israel's future will be the focus of the next chapter.

Summary of Chapter Ten

- Antichrist's empire will encompass the ancient boundaries of Rome's empire, even while Russia and the kings of the east assemble gigantic armies for Armageddon. Roman conquests, as foreseen by Daniel, absorbed the previous lands of the Egyptian, Medo-Persian, and Babylonian empires. Antichrist is therefore in "good company" to perform "bad tyranny."

- The False Prophet will be especially skilled at proclaiming Antichrist as the true Christ, a horrible mock and blasphemy. To mock more perfectly the ministries of John the Baptist and Elijah in their offices as Christ's forerunners, it is likely that the False Prophet will triumph during the biblical festival at Passover, by annunciating Antichrist as a resurrected Messiah with fire from the sky. A demonically-empowered image and deception and fire raining from the sky will help empower the False Prophet in deceiving millions.

- The False Prophet brings "life" to Antichrist's image. This event will usher in a momentous decision for each Jewish person worshipping God at the temple in Jerusalem. Should they bow before Antichrist's image or flee Antichrist as an idolater and blasphemer?
- "Father Satan," "Antichrist the Son," and "the spiritual false prophet" mock with exactness the glorious triune God who exists in Father, Son, and Holy Spirit.
- "Minor" Bible details count in any study of prophecy—Antichrist's "confirming" the covenant of Daniel 9:27 indicates that a covenant, secret or opened, was *already formed* when he "confirms."

The "144,000" are Not Christians!

What is the significance of a biblical "seal"? Ancient documents were sealed to protect their contents and to verify their authenticity. Scrolled documents were rolled closed, while shorter official papers would be folded and then tied and knotted closed. A lump of clay or softened wax would be placed over the knot. The author of the document could press into the hardening clay or wax a signet ring's mark or roll into the supple material with a cylindrical sealing device. The receiver of such a document was thus assured of the sender's authenticity and that its contents had not been tampered with in any way. For a king or governmental ruler, their seal signified all the authority and power of their realm.

An official seal was placed on the tomb of Jesus Christ. When the chief priests and Pharisees went to Pontius Pilate following Jesus' crucifixion, they enlisted aid in securing the tomb where Jesus was placed. Pilate replied to their request by sending a guard of Roman soldiers to the tomb (Matthew 27:65). He also urged them to consider how to make the tomb as secure as possible. A seal would have been placed on the stone blocking entrance to the tomb. The tomb's seal in addition to the fierce Roman guard notified the people that all the power and authority of Rome protected its precious contents.

> Then I saw another angel coming up from the east, having the seal of the living God. He called in a loud voice to the four angels who had been given power to harm the land and the sea. "Do not harm the land or the sea or the trees until we put a seal on the foreheads of the servants of our God." Then I heard the number of those who were sealed: 144,000 from all the tribes of Israel. Revelation 7:2–4

In the spiritual realm, the seal of the living God is a supernatural, or spiritual, mark. It signifies to angels and demons in the spirit realm that people on whom God has set His seal belong to and are protected by Him personally. The 144,000 persons of Revelation 11 are sealed before the sounding of the seven trumpets by seven angels. The sealing of the 144,000 will mark and protect them, therefore, from judgments to come, which include the fifth trumpet's horrible plague of locusts up from the abyss (Revelation 9:1–4).

Why is Revelation a "double telling" of events? To understand the chronology of the events prophesied in Revelation, it is helpful to understand the format the ancient Hebrews used to account for their history. An excellent illustration of their scribal technique is the Genesis record of the creation. Genesis 1:1–2:3 is an orderly and progressive account of the creation week through day seven and God's Sabbath of rest. Genesis 2:4–25 then refers back to day six with specific details, and Genesis 3 moves forward again to the account of the fall of man. In other words, an overall view of the creation week is presented first, and then the specifics concerning the creation of man were written.

The chronology of the book of Revelation is easily understood in the light of this biblical storytelling technique. Up through the first six seals: 1) an overview of the seven-year period (or seventieth week of Daniel) is written. The seventh seal, 2) focuses on trumpet judgments of God—overviews with some detail of more events are shared before, 3) the chronology of judgments continues in Revelation 15, the outpouring of the seven last plagues of God's wrath. Therefore, Israel is the focus of Revelation 7:1–8 (the sealing of 144,000 from the twelve tribes), and then Israel is not directly referred to again until chapter 12.

Some who teach a pre-tribulation rapture believe that Revelation's sealed 144,000 are Messianic Jews who have previously trusted in Christ. In their view, the Church is absent from the tribulation so others, namely the 144,000, evangelize those saved during this perilous time. Have you ever considered that the 144,000 are not only theorized as witnessing believers in Christ but also as super evangelists? There are no corresponding verses in Scripture to confirm such an interpretation for Revelation 7!

What does Scripture teach clearly about the 144,000?

> Now it is God who makes both us and you stand firm in Christ. He anointed us, set His seal on us, and put His spirit in our heart as a deposit, guaranteeing what is to come. 2 Corinthians 1:21–22 (See also Ephesians 1:13.)

First, the 144,000 are sealed on their foreheads to be *identified* spiritually as belonging to and being protected by God. If these were *already* born-again believers in Christ as per the pre-tribulational viewpoint, they would *already* have been sealed.

Second, the biblical seal, or mark, can *protect* those who refuse idolatry. The image of the beast in the temple will provoke the Lord to jealousy (Exodus 20:5) and result in the outpouring of His wrath upon the earth. Previous temple idolatry provoked jealousy and God destroyed Jerusalem and the temple by the Babylonians (Ezekiel 8:3).

Nebuchadnezzer exiled Ezekiel to Babylon eleven years before the devastation of the city and the temple. The son of a priest, Ezekiel was called by God to be a prophet in captivity. In the sixth year of his exile, Ezekiel was transported by the Holy Spirit to see Jerusalem. Ezekiel saw the abominable practices of the inhabitants of Jerusalem and a vision of six city guards (God's angels) and a seventh person, a man, clothed in linen with a writing kit at his side. The man told Ezekiel to, "Go throughout the city of Jerusalem and put a mark on the forehead of those who grieve and lament over the detestable things that are done in it" (Ezekiel 9:4).

What is the difference between the "mark" of God's seal, as in Ezekiel and Revelation, and the mark of the beast?

People unable to write their own names will often sign documents by making their mark, an X or another single letter. The word used for "mark" in the Hebrew Bible is the last letter of the Hebrew alphabet, a *tau*. The ancient Hebrew tau resembles an *x* or cross. The spiritual mark on the foreheads of those who lamented because of idolatry in the temple (as in Ezekiel 9:4) was a cruciform shape! The purpose of the Ezekiel mark was to protect the righteous from the wrath of God.

> For God did not appoint us (believers) to suffer wrath but to receive salvation through our Lord Jesus Christ. 1 Thessalonians 5:9

Believers in Jesus Christ will not suffer God's coming wrath. The 144,000 are sealed, protecting them from the coming wrath, just as a faithful remnant were marked in Ezekiel 9, saved from the judgment then to come. If the 144,000 were *already* in Christ as believers, as in the pre-tribulational view, they would not need what would then be a *second* sealing in Revelation 7 because they would be exempt from God's wrath to start!

The Jewish people will be on Earth at the time that God's wrath is completed. When the seventh angel sounds his trumpet on Rosh Hashanah, the Church is raptured, but the nation of Israel is left behind. In other words, the seal of God will protect 144,000 of His remnant people as the seven bowls are poured out upon the earth and its inhabitants.

A third reason the 144,000 cannot be "super evangelists" is that the good news is designated to be taken to the Jewish people and to all gentile nations (Matthew 28:19). Israel as the 144,000 would have difficulty bringing the gospel to all nations while she is isolated in seclusion, under fire from the Antichrist and desperately avoiding his wrath in hiding.

What is a possible interpretation of the Sun, Moon, and stars sign in Revelation?

> A great and wondrous sign appeared in heaven: a woman clothed with the sun, with the moon under her feet and a crown of twelve stars on her head. Revelation 12:1

Joseph, the favorite son of Israel/Jacob, dreamt the Sun, Moon, and eleven stars bowed to him (Genesis 37:9). The Sun and Moon represented Joseph's father and stepmother, Jacob and Leah. The eleven stars were Jacob's other male children. Note the similarities to Revelation 12:1. The woman crowned with twelve stars is the twelve-tribe nation of Israel, descended from the twelve sons of Jacob.

> The woman was given the two wings of a great eagle, so that she might fly to the place prepared for her in the desert, where she would be taken care of for a time, times and a half time, out of the serpent's reach. Revelation 12:14

The expression "on eagle's wings" is an idiom that means "quickly" (see Exodus 19:4). Antichrist's armies will pursue Israel as Jewish people with a heart for God flee the temple and the city. They will be cared for over three and a half years, out of Satan's reach. At that time:

> From His mouth the serpent spewed water like a river, to overtake the woman and sweep her away with the torrent. But the earth helped the woman by opening its mouth and swallowing the river that the dragon had spewed out of His mouth. Then the dragon was enraged at the woman and went off to make war against the rest of her offspring—those who obey God's commandments and hold to the testimony of Jesus. Revelation 12:15–17

The four beasts emerging from the churning sea in Daniel 7:3 were nations demonstrating strength and ferocity like that of wild, carnivorous animals. The churning sea symbolizes wicked humanity. Rivers supply the seas with fresh reserves of water—as a sea bolsters a river, fresh human troops bolster a conquering nation's army. The serpent of Revelation 12 is Satan, who empowers rulers of empires. "The serpent spewed water like a river" is a spiritual picture of Antichrist ordering troops to pursue Israel. The command is not only to pursue but destroy all the people (sweep "her" away). The woman carried away on eagle's wings is reminiscent of God's deliverance of Israel out of Egyptian bondage. Just as Pharaoh commanded troops to pursue and destroy Israel as they fled into the wilderness, so will the Antichrist issue similar orders against fleeing Israel.

How is Antichrist thwarted in his attempt to destroy the Jewish people?

"But if the LORD brings about something totally new, and the earth swallows them, with everything that belongs to them, and they go down alive into the grave, then you will know that these men have treated the LORD with contempt." Numbers 16:30

When Israel was in the wilderness, Korah, Dathan, and Abiram led a rebellion against Moses and Aaron, God's chosen leaders. These wicked men challenged the anointed prophet and high priest of the Lord. Rebellious, they, along with their households and possessions, went down alive to their graves and the earth then closed over them (Numbers 16:33–34). Treating the anointed of God with contempt is, biblically speaking, considered as treating God Himself with contempt. Those who pursue the sealed 144,000 are seeking to destroy God's sealed and chosen servants (Revelation 7:3). To protect the 144,000, the earth will open to swallow the Antichrist's soldiers alive. The Antichrist will be frustrated in his attempt to destroy Israel. Israel's protection is guaranteed for the duration of Antichrist's reign of terror.

Some scholars believe Israel will find a refuge in Petra (Greek for *rock*). (King David fled from the pursuing Saul and Saul's men by going down to a "rock" [see 1 Samuel 23:25]). The city of Petra was the capital of the Edomites, a notable fortress and stronghold. Petra achieved instant fame through the movie, *Indiana Jones and the Last Crusade*. The exterior shots of the film showing Indiana and his team at the Holy Grail crusaders' fortress were filmed at the ancient Petra stronghold, located in modern-day Jordan.

God our rock, our fortress, and our deliverer (Psalm 18:2) will protect Israel though the nations of the world will gather against her. Referring to Israel's future military deliverance, God tells us:

"On that day, when all the nations of the earth are gathered against her, I will make Jerusalem an immovable rock for all the nations." Zechariah 12:3

Zechariah refers to "that day" five more times in chapter 12. That day is known as the "great and terrible day of the LORD" (Zephaniah 1:14–18). This will be a terrible day when God tramples out the vintage of His wrath upon those who have gathered against His chosen people. This will be the day when the armies of the nations of the world have gathered in the plain of Megiddo for the final battle of Armageddon. This will be the day when Jesus Christ returns, a sharp sword in His mouth used to strike the nations (Revelation 19:15).

How does the description of the 144,000 help confirm that they are religious and not Messianic Jews? The 144,000 are described as "those who did not defile themselves with women, for they kept themselves pure" (Revelation 14:4a). Many interpret this description to mean that the 144,000 are celibates and virgins, either natural (never having had physical relations) or spiritual (never having been defiled by idolatry). I agree that the passage can be taken in the spiritual sense of purity.

On the other hand, there is a natural interpretation to this passage when we understand that the 144,000 are unsaved Jews. In order for these men to participate in the renewed temple worship and sacrifice, they would have to refrain from sexual relationships, even with their wives (according to Leviticus 15:16–17, an emission of semen renders a person ceremonially unclean). In the middle of the seven, sacrifice and offering are halted by the Antichrist. When they are told to bow before the image of the Antichrist, the eyes of these men are opened. They are then sealed to protect them from the coming judgment and they flee the temple.

As we have discussed thus far in *The Last Days Calendar,* the Church is raptured, I believe, at the biblical Feast of Trumpets. There are then ten days left between the Feast of Trumpets (Rosh HaShona/the Jewish New Year) and Yom Kippur, Day of Atonement. Religiously observant Jews know these ten days as the Ten Days of Awe.

Between Rosh HaShona and Yom Kippur, Jewish people world-wide wonder, will their names be inscribed in the book of life for the coming year? Will they live through the coming year and have life in Heaven besides? The biblical relationship I perceive between the literal Day of Atonement and the literal time of Christ's return will be explored in exciting detail in our next chapter.

Summary of Chapter Eleven

- Revelation 7:4 is among the most commonly misunderstood Scripture verses. The 144,000 are not the sole 144,000 people permitted in Heaven as the Jehovah's Witnesses suggest. Neither are they gentile Christians, as replacement theologians (who believe in error that God has cast aside Israel from His care and covenants) suggest. They are also not super evangelists who reach the world for Christ during the tribulation, with the Church absent and raptured! They are instead:

    o Jewish people from the twelve tribes of Israel as Revelation 7:4 plainly states
    o Marked by God for their protection, as they have a zeal for God but are not yet born-again believers in Jesus Christ
    o "Set aside" to endure the Great Tribulation with the Jewish people, probably in Petra, while the gentile nations suffer at the hands of Antichrist's warfare and destruction

- In other words, the "144,000" of Revelation are not Christians at the time of their sealing. To replace the literal Jews of Revelation 7, marked for their abiding faith in God, with

New Testament believers is a hallmark of cults, including Mormonism and the Jehovah's Witness movement.

- Revelation is completely chronological in its storytelling, a "two-telling" of events, like the Genesis account, which contains two back-to-back accounts of the creation.
- Antichrist hates Jews and Christians alike and will war against the Jewish people, some of whom will successfully flee his wrath to the ancient Edomite fortress known as Petra.
- The Jewish people will be a stumbling block and destruction to the nations as they fight ferociously to defend their homeland on their day of deliverance. First, however, a terrible Day of Atonement—suffering and mourning—must take place as part of the Ten Days of Awe between the Jewish New Year and Day of Atonement.

Chapter 12

"These (!) are My Appointed Feasts"

The LORD said to Moses, "Speak to the Israelites and say to them: 'These are my appointed feasts, the appointed feasts of the LORD, which you are to proclaim as sacred assemblies.'"

—Leviticus 23:1–2

Bible critics commonly misunderstand the "many translations" the Bible has undergone, to imply the messages of the ancient prophets have been diluted or even twisted for modern day readers. The opposite is indeed true—though the Bible has been translated many times, most of those undertakings were done with a group of scholars making one switch—from the Scriptures' original languages straight into the *lingua franca* of the common people.

The first ever translation of the Old Testament, from its original Hebrew and Aramaic into Greek, is known as the Septuagint. What we call today the book of Leviticus receives its name from the Septuagint nomenclature and means, "relating to the Levites." Aaron and his sons were descended from the one of Jacob's twelve sons, Levi, and their family served Israel as priests. Temple workers who assisted in the duties related to worship and its regulations were also from the tribe of Levi. The book of Leviticus records God's laws and regulations concerning worship, ceremonial cleanness, morality, and the appointed feasts of God.

The first of the sacred assemblies listed in Leviticus 23, or "of the Levites 23," to be observed by Israel alone, is the Sabbath day of rest, a weekly sacred assembly. Seven annual feasts are then listed, the first four of them to be observed in the spring of each year. The Passover, Unleavened Bread, and Firstfruits all take place during Nisan, or Abib, the first month of the Hebrew ceremonial calendar. The closing festival of the spring cycle is the Feast of Weeks, also known as "Pentecost," which takes place during Sivan, the third month. There are no festivals during summer months, and other celebrations await harvest time each year.

> "Do you not say, 'Four more months and then the harvest'? I tell you, open your eyes and look at the fields! They are ripe for harvest." John 4:35 80

Jesus and His disciples traveled through Samaria and came to the town of Sychar. About noon one day, Jesus sat by a well and rested while His disciples went into town. Jesus spoke with a woman who had come to draw water from the well. His insight and spiritual understanding confirmed to her that He was a prophet. When the woman spoke about the coming of the Messiah, Jesus declared, "I who speak to you am he." Leaving her water jar behind, the woman sped back to her town and said to the people, "Come, see a man who told me everything I ever did. Could this be the Christ?" They came out of the town and made their way toward him.

Why did the woman at the well neglect to bring her jar home with her in her rush? His disciples, upon returning from town, were surprised to find their teacher talking with a woman, and a despised Samaritan at that! The Samaritans were a mixed race and viewed as perpetually unclean by the Israelites. The woman forgot to take home her earthen vessel made for filling with well water, because she sought instead to be an earthen, human vessel filled with the living water of God's Holy Spirit. As the town's people traveled back to the well with her to meet Jesus, He told His disciples to open their "spiritual eyes" to look upon fields ripe for a *harvest of souls*. The Samaritans, considered unclean and as Gentiles, were ready to receive Christ as Lord and Savior though they were not purely Jews in genealogy (see John 4:3–32).

What is the "harvest of souls" and the relationships between the great harvests of the Scriptures? Jesus declared to His disciples, "Do you not say, 'Four more months and then the harvest?'" (John 4:35).

The *barley* harvest takes place in the spring cycle of festivals. Starting with the Passover week, *four* distinct festival observances are observed, a source of confusion for many Bible scholars. The Passover festival, a picture of redemption through the blood of the true Lamb, Jesus Christ, begins at twilight on the fourteenth day of the month (Leviticus 23:5).

Next, the second Feast, the Feast of Unleavened Bread, picturing the holy life of the true believer freed of the death penalty of sin, begins on the fifteenth day of that month and lasts for seven days (Leviticus 23:6).

The third festival, the Feast of Firstfruits, includes a wave offering of a sheaf of barley held aloft and is observed the day following the Sabbath (Leviticus 23:11). Jesus Himself arose in His tomb early on the first day of the week, following the close of the Sabbath (Matthew 27:1–6). He resurrected therefore on the Feast of Firstfruits. Christ is therefore described by Paul as the "firstfruits of the resurrection" (1 Corinthians 15:22–23).

Fifty days after the Feast of *Firstfruits*, the Feast of *Weeks*, called Pentecost by the Church, takes place. The Feast of Weeks is a period of seven weeks plus one day (forty-nine days plus one day equals the fifty days of Pentecost). Pentecost means literally, "fifty." At the Pentecost, following Christ's resurrection, the Holy Spirit descended to Earth in power (Acts 2:1–4).

What about Pentecost and the wheat harvest is significant? Not to confuse you, dear reader, but Pentecost, or Feast of Weeks, is also the Day of Firstfruits of the *wheat harvest* (different from the Firstfruits of spring *barley harvest* mentioned above). Two wheat loaves became a wave offering before the Lord. Born-again believers in Christ are symbolized in Scripture as fruit of the wheat harvest, while those who reject Christ are referred to as chaff or weeds (Matthew 3:12; 13:24–30). A beautiful double picture—wheat is harvested and taken into a barn (believers gathered to Heaven) while chaff and weeds are tossed in a fire (eternal damnation for unbelievers). At Pentecost, after Christ's resurrection and ascension, the Church was "watered" by the Spirit and began to "grow." At the rapture, the Church will be "reaped and gathered together" to be with the Lord. There are four months from Pentecost until the fall cycle of biblical feasts.

How do the autumn festival days play out on the Hebrew calendar? The three fall festivals take place in the seventh month, Tishri. The three observances in fall are Rosh HaShona (Jewish New Year), Yom Kippur (Day of Atonement), and Sukkot (Feast of Tabernacles). I believe that on Rosh HaShona, celebrated on the first day of the seventh month, with the trumpet call of God, the dead in Christ will rise first followed by the living Christians at His coming, that is, the great rapture! (See 1 Thessalonians 4:16–17.)

Following the Exodus from Egypt, God commanded that the spring month of Nisan become the first month on the Hebrew calendar. Before the Exodus, the calendar started in the fall with the month of Tishri, which is why the New Year finds its way from the first to the seventh month of the Hebrew calendar. Jewish tradition holds to the belief that Rosh HaShona is the day that God began creation. When the trumpet sounds, the dead will be raised imperishable, and we, who are new creations in Christ, will be changed. We will receive new bodies (1 Corinthians 15:52; 2 Corinthians 5:17).

What about the mysterious, "hidden rapture theory"?

> I do not want you to be ignorant of this mystery, brothers, so that you may not be conceited: Israel has experienced a hardening in part until the full number of Gentiles has come in. And so all Israel will be saved, as it is written . . . Romans 11:25–26a

The uncircumcised Gentiles were excluded from citizenship in Israel and were foreigners to the first covenants of promise to Israel. Through the blood of Christ, however, Gentiles can be reconciled to God—fellow citizens with God's people and members of God's household (Ephesians 2:11–19). God's plan is to soften Israel's heart toward Him following His final judgment of Israel and judgment of the nations for their treatment of Israel. All Israel who remains alive following the tribulation will be saved (see Romans 11:26). At Rosh Hashanah, the surviving remnant of Israel will look and see Christ in the air as He triumphantly descends to earth in His *visible* procession:

> Look, he is coming with the clouds, and every eye will see him, even those who pierced him, and all the peoples of the earth will mourn because of him. So shall it be! Amen. Revelation 1:7

How is it that "every eye" (every one) will see the return of Christ? Is it through worldwide television broadcasting as some have suggested? I believe there is a simple and elegant solution to the question.

On a clear day, it would take but a moment for a person to look up into the sky and see the brightness of the noonday Sun. For all to see the noonday Sun on a particular sunny day, therefore, it would take twenty-four hours—the earth making one complete rotation upon its axis—and all of Earth's inhabitants could see the Sun directly overhead at noon in their time zone.

Before Christ's coming in the air, the Sun will blacken to the color of sackcloth and the Moon will turn blood red (Revelation 6:12). (The earth, of course, will not only be in great physical darkness but in great spiritual darkness amongst its inhabitants.) With sunlight unseen, everyone could still see Jesus Christ coming in power and great glory (Matthew 24:29–30). As the elect are gathered from the four winds to meet the Lord in the air, the Sun of Righteousness (see Malachi 4:2) will burn brightly over the earth all that day. Every eye would see the glory of God shine brighter than the noonday Sun, as Jesus, the very radiance of God's glory, shatters the darkness in His coming in the air for His Church. Even blind persons would be able to feel such radiance on the corneas of sightless eyes!

Are there precedents in Jewish tradition for tying the Jewish New Year to the return of Christ? In the Jewish tradition, Rosh HaShona is the day of God's annual judgment, when God opens the book of life for the coming new year. The observant Jew holds to the notion that God will finish His decisions some days later, sealing up the book of life on Yom Kippur, the Day of Atonement. The Feast of Trumpets/Rosh HaShona is observed on the first day of the seventh month. Ten days later in that month is the Day of Atonement. This ten-day period between these appointed observances is known as the Ten Days of Penitence, or the Ten Days of Awe. It is widely believed that the Ten Days of Penitence is an opportune time to obtain God's pardon and be inscribed in the book of life for the coming year. Jewish thought maintains that one can merit God's favor through fasting, increased prayer, Torah study, and good works during this ten-day period. What could happen during the Ten Days of Awe framing Christ's return?

> "I will pour out on the house of David and the inhabitants of Jerusalem a spirit of grace and supplication. They will look on me, the one they have pierced and they will mourn for him as one mourns for an only child, and grieve bitterly for him as one grieves for a firstborn son." Zechariah 12:10

If the Church is raptured on Rosh HaShona to meet a glorious Christ in the air (not a "secret rapture" as portrayed in popular Christian media), the Jewish people would literally look upon the one their leaders had pierced on the cross through conspiracy with Rome, astonished at their rejection of Messiah to open the days of awe and days of repentance. Christ will rapture His Church away for both judgments as to rewards and to celebrate at the marriage supper of the Lamb (Revelation 11:18; 19:9).

> "How awful that day will be! It will be a time of trouble for Jacob, but he will be saved out of it." Jeremiah 30:7

The Lord will pour out His spirit of grace upon the remnant of Israel on those who have survived the tribulation, "Jacob's trouble," soon after.

Jacob is the father of the twelve tribes of Israel. God's spirit of grace upon the surviving remnant from the twelve tribes indicates that Jacob's people in the future will be saved both physically and spiritually. A spirit of supplication will drive Israel to her knees in desperate and fervent prayer during the Ten Days of Awe. She will mourn because the true Messiah of Israel came only for those in the Church, Jews and Gentiles, and now is gone again soon after! Israel will be on Earth during the pouring out of the last seven plagues. All Israel will be saved, but the promise to redeem corporate, national Israel would not have occurred until the Day of Atonement. The Day of Atonement, the most solemn day of the Hebrew ceremonial calendar, is distinct and unique today among all the days of the year. Let's examine the Day of Atonement more closely.

The Torah, which consists of The Five Books of Moses (the Pentateuch), contains numerous regulations for corporate worship. From Moses' day until the building of the temple by Solomon, worship was conducted in a movable sanctuary, a tabernacle. In the front room for the tabernacle stood a lampstand, a table, and consecrated bread in an area called the Holy Place. Behind a curtain was a sanctuary called the Most Holy Place (see Hebrews 9:2–3).

Israelite priests participated in daily sacrifices, offerings, the burning of incense, and the bestowing of priestly blessings. The priests entered regularly into the Holy Place in their course of their duties. Only the high priest could enter into the Most Holy Place or Holy of Holies, and only once yearly, on the Day of Atonement:

> Only the high priest entered the inner room, and that only once a year, and never without blood, which he offered for himself and for the sins the people had committed in ignorance. Hebrews 9:7

In the Most Holy Place, the glorious presence of the living God covered the mercy seat of the ark of God's covenant. For the high priest to unwittingly enter into the Most Holy Place without a blood covering for sin would result in his immediate death! Further, the high priest first had to offer acceptable blood atonement for himself and his household (Leviticus 16:6) before he could offer blood upon the altar on behalf of the rest of Israel.

The Day of Atonement regulations therefore include an offering for unintentional sin. These would include sins committed in ignorance, due to haste or through sinful carelessness. The offering for unintentional sin is linked to the regular sacrificial system of the rest of the year. Most Bible readers do not realize that the standard sacrificial system atoned solely for unintentional sins!

With the exception of the Day of Atonement offering, there was no other provision for atonement for sin of wickedness and rebellion, lust or pride, indeed, any sin not committed in ignorance of God's law. The Day of Atonement offering covered "transgression" (sin committed when the offending sinner knows consciously or by law code that their action is evil). Intentional sin is rooted in a heart rebellious toward God:

> "When Aaron has finished making atonement for the Most Holy Place, the Tent of Meeting and the altar, he shall bring forward the live goat. He is to lay both hands on the head of the live goat and confess over it all the wickedness and rebellion of the Israelites—all their sins—and put them on the goat's head." Leviticus 16:20–21a

The high priest first offered a bull to make atonement for himself and his family and household each Yom Kippur. Then, taking two live male goats, a lot was cast, determining which goat would be slaughtered and the sin offering to the Lord, and which would be the scapegoat, presented alive to the Lord and the congregation. The blood of the slaughtered goat was sprinkled on the mercy seat of the ark in the Most Holy Place. Blood from this goat was also sprinkled over the Holy Place and upon the horns of the sacrificial altar. These places stood defiled by the intentional sin of Israel.

Taking the living goat, the high priest placed his hands on its head and confessed the sins of Israel over it. All the sins of Israel, including wickedness and rebellion, were considered transferred to this literal "scapegoat." The scapegoat was released into the desert to wander and die. The scapegoat's Hebrew name is *Azazel*, which has been considered a title for Satan. The desert with its barren wilderness symbolizes the place of eternal judgment for wicked and rebellious man, apart from trusting in Christ:

> "All the nations will be gathered before him, and he will separate the people one from another as a shepherd separates the sheep from the goats. He will put the sheep on His right and the goats on His left." Matthew 25:32–33

> "Then he will say to those on His left, 'Depart from me, you who are cursed, into eternal fire prepared for the devil and His angels.'" Matthew 25:41

Yom Kippur, the Day of Atonement, is the sole day on the Hebrew calendar when atonement is made for sin of wickedness and rebellion. Note in context that the ultimate rejection of Jesus Christ by the nation of Israel was not a sin committed in ignorance or haste but was willful and intentional.

How was the intentional rejection of Jesus by the Pharisees enacted?

> Now there was a man of the Pharisees named Nicodemus, a member of the Jewish ruling council. He came to Jesus at night and said, "Rabbi, we know you are a teacher who has come from God. For no one could perform the miraculous signs you are doing if God were not with him." John 3:1–2

Nicodemus, a Pharisee, confirmed what the ruling council knew—that Jesus performed His many miracles by the power of God. Jesus affirmed that He was a true prophet of God by the "lawful double proof" (two witnesses confirm a fact according to the Scriptures) of: 1) performing miracles, and 2) His evidenced devotion to the heavenly Father. (See Deuteronomy 13:1–4 for a comparison to Christ's faithful walk with the Father.)

Nicodemus knew all Israel was astonished that Jesus was able to cast a demon from a man who was blind and mute. To exorcise a demon it was considered necessary to know the name or title of the possessing demon. (Since a mute cannot speak, it was firmly believed that only the true Messiah could perform such a miracle.) Indeed, the Talmud marks this specific miracle as affirming the identity of the true Jewish Messiah. When Jesus attested to His Messiahship by performing this wondrous sign, the people turned to the Pharisees and said: "Could this not be the Son of David (Messiah)?" (Matthew 12:22–23).

Had the Pharisees answered the question truthfully, the people would have crowned Jesus as King Messiah. Instead, with full complicity, they lied and blasphemed, saying that Jesus was empowered to do miracles by Satan. The nation at this time committed the sin of blaspheming God's Holy Spirit and that generation stood condemned. Immediately following that act of rebellion, Jesus no longer preached so the masses could receive the message of salvation but spoke in parables, saying privately to His disciples, "The knowledge of the secrets of the kingdom of heaven has been given to you, but not to them" (Matthew 13:11).

In fulfillment of prophecy, the masses in Jerusalem would see miracles and hear truth, yet not comprehend it accurately because Israel's heart had become callused (Isaiah 6:9–10; Matthew 13:13–15). The rejection of the Christ by the nation of Israel, with the exception of a "called out" remnant of Jewish believers, meant that the message of salvation would go to the Gentiles instead, making Israel and her priests envious (Romans 11:11). But the good news of God's kindness and mercy awaits all Israel in the future!

If Israel as a nation rejected Jesus, when will Israel accept their Messiah nationwide?

> For if their rejection is the reconciliation of the world, what will their acceptance be but life from the dead? Romans 11:15

Examine carefully this scenario: Israel's redemption traditionally takes place on the Day of Atonement. All of Israel's sins must be forgiven, including wickedness and rebellion, to bring all members of Israel (the Jewish people as a whole) to salvation as in Romans 11:26. According to God's regulations concerning appointed days, sins of the nation are pardoned only on the Day of Atonement.

The rapture entails both the transformation of the living saints and the resurrection of those who have died as believers in Christ. Since the resurrection of the dead precedes the translation of those who are alive at His coming, without life first from the dead, there is no rapture for the living. Is Romans 11:15 closely associating Israel's acceptance of Christ with the rapture of the blessed dead? If so, since Israel in Revelation's chronology does not find full salvation until the near end of the tribulation, the rapture cannot be a pre-tribulation event!

The next chapter will address the backdrop of conditions on the earth when God pours out His wrath. What will happen to the nations surrounding Israel is addressed.

Summary of Chapter Twelve

- God's calendar for the fulfillment of prophecy is always an exact one. Following the mention of the Sabbath in Leviticus 23, four spring festivals are described that have been prominent in the history of Israel and the story of the Church:

  o   The Passover with the slaying of the lamb
  o   The Feast of Unleavened Bread

- o The Feast of Firstfruits, coincident with the *barley* harvest
- o The Feast of Weeks, coincident with the first of the *wheat* harvest

- Three more observances occur in the fall, in the seventh month of the Hebrew calendar:

  - o Rosh HaShona, the Jewish New Year/Feast of Trumpets
  - o Yom Kippur, Day of Atonement
  - o Sukkot, the Feast of Tabernacles

- The time period between the New Year and Day of Atonement is know as the Days of Awe, and this time is intimately bound with ultimate atonement, repentance, and redemption in biblical and traditional Jewish thought. The Bible seems to indicate that the Days of Awe are likewise intimately associated with Israel's redemption at Christ's Second Coming.
- God's "harvests of human souls" are linked to the agricultural harvests of the Hebrew ceremonial calendar. We have every biblical reason to expect future prophetic events, including the rapture, the military and spiritual salvation of Israel, and even Christ's triumphant return, to coincide with corresponding festival days of the Bible, just as Christ died during a festival, lay in the tomb during a festival, rose during a festival, preached His Messiahship during a festival celebration (John 10), was born on a festival, etc.
- Romans 11, explaining that all Israel will receive salvation, refers to all Jewish people alive at the close of the tribulation, not the Church as "spiritual Israel" or the Church re-

placing Israel's promises in God's scheme of things. Replacement theology is grave doctrinal error and undermines a clear understanding of biblical prophecy as fulfilled by future literal events.

- Christ's return processional at the rapture will be as evident as the shining of the noonday Sun, therefore, "every eye" will see Him, without the benefit of television cameras.

- The rapture of the Church is closely aligned with both horrible judgments and great deliverance for Israel. Since Israel's hope is revealed near the close of the tribulation, the pre-tribulation rapture view is unsupported by the Scriptures. (This book is not advocating a post-tribulation rapture, either, as will be discussed in following chapters!)

- Yom Kippur, Day of Atonement, is the sole provision in Old Testament law for atonement of intentional sin by individuals and corporate Israel, a nation under a theocracy. It seems logical, therefore, to place a visible, resplendent rapture of the Church on a Sun-blackened Day of Atonement, ushering in tremendous sorrow and repentance for the Jewish people—followed by tremendous redemption and restoration of Israel at the dawn of her Millennial Age and Christ's reign on Earth.

- As we shall see in subsequent chapters, placing the rapture and Christ's return on a ceremonial festival day is not guilty against the Lord's "date setting" admonition of Matthew 25:13: "Therefore keep watch, because you do not know the day or the hour."

Chapter 13

As in Noah's Day

"As it was in the days of Noah, so it will be at the coming of the Son of Man." Matthew 24:36

If He condemned the cities of Sodom and Gomorrah by burning them to ashes, and made them an example of what is going to happen to the ungodly; and if he rescued Lot, a righteous man, who was distressed by the filthy lives of lawless men . . .

—2 Peter 2:6–7

The worldwide flood of Noah's day is a picture of the completion of God's wrath, which occurs in the days when the seventh angel is about to sound the seventh trumpet. Seven golden bowls filled with God's wrath are poured upon the earth (Revelation 15:7) and its wicked inhabitants. These final plagues are an outpouring of punishments in the natural realm, not to be confused with the final judgment of unbelievers to Hell. Sodom and Gomorrah engulfed in burning sulfur is a far better picture of the final judgment of those not trusting in Christ. Those who reject Christ die with their sin debt unpaid and will be cast in the lake of fire for eternity.

How does Noah represent a true picture of the time of the rapture? Noah and Lot, declared as righteous, were kept from suffering the punishment poured upon the *wicked of their generation*. Noah and Lot serve as examples of the elect in Christ kept from the hour of trial to come upon the world (Revelation 3:10).

Noah and his sons and Noah's spouse and his sons' wives entered the ark to escape the waters of the flood. Pairs of clean and unclean animals, birds, and all terrestrial creatures, male and female, came to enter the ark, and the floodwaters covered the earth (see Genesis 7:7–10).

Noah's ark was the provision to escape the coming outpouring of God's wrath. The Hebrew word for atonement is *kapar*. It means literally, "covering." Noah's ark was covered with a coating of pitch, making it a watertight craft. Following Noah's time in a similar vein, the Mosaic Law had sin "temporarily covered" by the blood of sacrificed animals. *Kapar* contains the same consonants as the quite similar word *koper*, which is translated as "pitch." The pitch covering protected Noah and his family from the floodwaters of judgment as surely as believers are protected from God's final wrath by the atoning blood of Jesus Christ.

Noah's family took their refuge in the ark. The believer finds refuge in Christ. Noah's refuge aboard the ark is a type or picture of the rapture, God's provision to protect His Church from the final hour of trial. He will rapture the elect and then pour the bowls of His wrath upon the earth just as wrath was poured upon the inhabitants of the earth in Noah's time:

> Pairs of all creatures that have the breath of life in them came to Noah and entered the ark. The animals going in were male and female of every living thing, as God had commanded Noah. Then the LORD shut him in. Genesis 7:15–16

Corrupt men filled with violence characterized Noah's time. Noah's neighbors were a wicked generation, and the thoughts of men ran continually to evil. Wickedness and perversity also describe the generation who will witness the Second Coming of Christ. The unsaved masses, self-centered and focused upon fleshly things (2 Timothy 3:1–4) will be unaware of coming judgment until it pours upon them like the Noahic flood (Matthew 24:38–39).

In Noah's time there was a special period of one week, followed immediately by the outpouring of the flood. During this week, the eight humans and the animals traveled to Noah. They then rested in God's provision for salvation from the flood, the great ark, and it was closed tightly by God against others entering in. This seven-day period of time has been correlated, mistakenly, I believe, with a pre-tribulation rapture. In the final days of this age there will indeed be a period of "seven" terminated with the outpouring of God's wrath—and the door to the wedding feast of the Lamb will then be closed tightly—but note that Noah's ark was not spirited away from evil like Enoch and Ezekiel were but remained on the earth—others enabled to enter in, firmly in place in the midst of a wicked people!

If the ark was in place during the seven days of Noah's time, what of the other "arks" of the Bible? As discussed in chapters seven through ten of *The Last Days Calendar*, the interpretation of Daniel's vision of four beasts is that those creatures symbolize gentile empires. Acts records that the apostle Peter had a vision in which he also saw many creatures.

Peter was residing in the city of Joppa at the home of Simon the tanner. Many homes in the ancient Middle East had outdoor stairways leading to a flat roof. Peter ascended one such stairway to a roof to pray. Becoming hungry and wanting something to eat while a meal was being prepared downstairs, Peter fell into a trance. He saw Heaven open and something resembling a large heavenly sheet brought to earth by its four corners. The sheet contained a wide variety of animals, including reptiles and birds. A voice spoke to Peter, commanding, "Get up, Peter. Kill and eat." (See Acts 10:10–13.)

Peter protested the command from Heaven because, according to Mosaic Law, Jews are forbidden to eat ceremonially unclean animals, including some of the animals on the sheet. The voice from Heaven responded that no thing is considered impure that God has made to be clean. Three times Peter protested and three times the voice responded. While Peter wondered about the interpretation of what he had seen and experienced, three men approached him, and he snapped out of his reverie. Cornelius, a devout Gentile, had sent the men. Peter, an apostle with a special calling to his Jewish people, had been called in a dream and by the three men to travel to Caesarea, to dine at the house of an "unclean Gentile." Peter was to share the message of salvation with this Roman centurion and his family.

Talking with Cornelius, Peter went inside his home and found a large gathering of people there. He told them:

> "You are well aware that it is against our law for a Jew to associate with a Gentile or visit him. But God has shown me that I should not call any man impure or unclean." Acts 10:27–28

The diverse animals Peter saw in his vision symbolized the gentile nations. Although Peter saw both clean and unclean animals in his vision, God had demonstrated to Peter not to call any *person* whom God can save impure or unclean. Certainly, the sheet filled with animals, held at the corners, would form an ark-like shape in Peter's vision.

How do Bible types explain the timing of the rapture? There is a symbolic picture that can be drawn from the biblical record of pairs of clean and unclean animals: *"every creature that has the breath of life in it"* entering Noah's ark for seven days. It is a picture of Jews and Gentiles, "clean and unclean" people, with the Holy Spirit (the breath of new life) in them, joining the Church over seven years before the rapture closes the salvation door.

The floodwaters came upon the earth *after* the seven days elapsed. On that seventh day, the Lord shut everyone in the ark (Genesis 7:16). On the day the Lord's wrath is to be poured out, on that very day, the Church will be lifted away from the earth.

In Noah's time, the ancient world was deluged, destroyed due to man's wickedness. Later, during the life of Abraham, God again punished sin by destroying the wicked cities of the plain of Jordan. The Lord sent two avenging angels ahead to Sodom while He remained behind to reveal His plan to Abraham:

> Then Abraham approached him and said, "Will you sweep away the righteous with the wicked? What if there are fifty righteous people in the city? Will you really sweep it away and not spare the place for the sake of fifty righteous people in it?" Genesis 18:23–24

The Lord replied that, certainly, He would certainly spare the city for the sake of fifty righteous people. Abraham continued to plead with the Lord on behalf of Sodom and its inhabitants. In mercy, God agreed to spare the city for the sake of forty-five or forty or thirty or twenty or even ten believing people. Ten righteous men, a small number indeed for a city, were not found, and the cities of Sodom and Gomorrah and the entire plain of Jordan were incinerated with burning sulfur. Only Abraham's nephew Lot would be found righteous, his household spared.

With the coming of dawn following Sodom's judgment, *the angels* urged Lot, saying:

"Hurry! Take your wife and your two daughters who are here, or you will be swept away when the city is punished.' When he hesitated, the men grasped His hand and the hands of His wife and of His two daughters and led them safely out of the city, for the LORD was merciful to them." Genesis 19:15–16

Sodom pictures the sinful world in which only God's grace saves believers. The Lord was merciful to Lot and His family. *The deliverance of righteous Lot is a type of the rapture.* Angels will gather the elect before the outpouring of the seven bowls of God's wrath. On the very day Lot was pulled from Sodom, judgment rained upon the city. On the very day of the rapture, the seven last plagues will begin to be poured upon the earth:

For the LORD himself will come down from heaven, with a loud command, with the voice of the archangel and with the trumpet call of God, and the dead in Christ will rise first. After that, we who are still alive and are left will be caught up together with them in the clouds to meet the LORD in the air. And so we will be with the LORD forever. 1 Thessalonians 4:16–17

Many of those who embrace a pre-tribulation rapture view believe the rapture is a secret event. In such a view, the elect in Christ only hear the loud command and call of God. A secret rapture is contrary to the clear teaching of Scripture that states that every eye will see Jesus at His appearing in the air (Revelation 1:7), unless the coming of Christ happens over several disparate stages, an awkwardness that pre-tribulation scholars admit. Is it not logical that the rapture will be an event of biblical proportions emphasized by a worldwide demonstration of the power and glory of the Lord? It seems as though the rapture will be heralded by the glorious presence of Christ, a thunderous shout, the booming voice of the archangel, and trumpet blasts heard around the globe. There will be such a cacophony of sound and such an authoritative command from the Lord that the dead in Christ shall be raised to life!

A fine example of the "trumpet blast" of the rapture is seen in the famous story of Jericho's walls: On the seventh day of Joshua's marching campaign at Jericho, the people awoke at daybreak and marched around the city seven times. The seventh time around, when the priests sounded the trumpet blasts, Joshua commanded the people, "Shout! For the LORD has given you the city!" (See Joshua 6:15–16.)

When Joshua was a youth he was named *Hoshea* (see Numbers 13:8–16). Hoshea is a Hebrew word translated as "salvation" in English. Later Moses changed Hoshea's name to Joshua, meaning, "The Lord saves."

Mary and Joseph were told separately by an angel that Mary would give birth to a son despite her virginity. They were commanded to name the child Jesus (Matthew 1:20–21; Luke 1:30–31). "Jesus" is taken from the Hebrew name for Joshua. Joshua, who led his people to victories in the Promised Land, is a picture of Jesus Christ.

The day Jericho fell to the Israelites, all the nation of Israel awaited Joshua's orders. As the trumpets sounded, Joshua issued a loud command and the people shouted in response. When the great city wall collapsed, the men of Israel charged into the city, putting every living thing within to death. Only Rahab the prostitute and her household were spared. The battle of Jericho foreshadows the rapture and Christ's return to Earth. Joshua is a type of Christ, accompanied by trumpet blasts and a shouted command also. Complete victory, including the slaughter in Jericho, resembled Christ and His armies treading the vineyard of God's fury (see Revelation 19:11–15). Israel, who has committed spiritual harlotry by worshipping idols in past, will be spared, as were the harlot Rahab and her family.

What do the seven days of Jericho have in common with Daniel's period of "seven?"

"He will confirm a covenant for one 'seven'." Daniel 9:27a

Then the LORD said to Joshua, "See, I have delivered Jericho into your hands, along with its king and its fighting men. March around the city once with all your armed men. Do this for six days. Have seven priests carry trumpets of rams' horns in front of the ark. On the seventh day, march around the city seven times, with the priests blowing trumpets." Joshua 6:2–4

Since the battle of Jericho foreshadows elements connected with Daniel's seventieth week, we must make a distinction between the first six days of the siege of Jericho and the final day of victory in battle.

Since the term seven in Daniel 9 represents a seven-year period, it is understood that each day of Daniel's week symbolizes a one-year period. The first six days of the battle of Jericho parallel the first six years of Daniel's "seven."

As an aside, it is fascinating to note that Jericho was built upon an elliptically-shaped mound of land. Our solar year is the amount of time it takes the earth to complete one orbit around the Sun, on an elliptically-shaped path. Once each day, for six days, the army of Israel marched around the walled city of Jericho in a path resembling Earth's celestial one-year orbit about the Sun . . .

On the seventh day of their march, Joshua's procession circled Jericho seven times while seven priests blew seven ram's horn trumpets. The ram's horn is blown at each new moon (Psalm 81:3) and announces the first day of each new month. The Moon revolves around the earth once each month. I believe that each of the seven times Israel marched around Jericho to the sounds of trumpets correspond to a month-long period in Revelation, totaling seven months in all. The seven priests blowing seven trumpets of rams' horns stands parallel to the account in Revelation of seven angels sounding seven trumpets (Revelation 8:6). I further surmise that since the ram's horn is blown at the new moon festival that Revelation's angels will sound their trumpets on the first day of each month in the Hebrew calendar.

> The LORD said to Moses and Aaron in Egypt, "This is to be for you the first month of your year." Exodus 12:1–2

> The first angel sounded His trumpet, and there came hail and fire mixed with blood, and it was hurled down upon the earth. Revelation 8:7a

The Lord proclaimed the seventh month, Nisan, the month of the Passover (deliverance from Egyptian bondage) as the new first month of the Hebrew calendar. (It is interesting to note the close parallels between the plagues of Egypt and the plagues associated with the sounding of the first trumpet by the first angel.) If the first angel sounds a trumpet on the first day of the first month and so on, we can conclude that this progression continues until the seventh angel sounds a trumpet on the first day of Tishri—the day Rosh HaShona is observed. The day of the Feast of Trumpets would then coincide with the sounding of the seventh and last trumpet!

> Listen, I tell you a mystery: We will not all sleep, but we will all be changed—in a flash, in the twinkling of an eye, at the last trumpet. 1 Corinthians15:52a

When is the last trumpet sounded? Paul wrote to the Corinthians as though they knew when the last trumpet made its blast in the Hebrew calendar. The biblical accounts of the Noahic flood, Sodom and Gomorrah's destruction, and the battle of Jericho, indicate in picture form that the rapture may take place in the seventh month of the seventh year of Daniel's seventieth week. This would not be a secret event but surely one of the most dramatic and witnessed events in world history.

Summary of Chapter Thirteen

- The author agrees with pre-tribulation rapture scholars who understand Noah's ark as a powerful picture of the believer's protection from God's wrath. God's wrath seems to fall coincident with the sounding of the seventh trumpet of Revelation, however, and a careful study of Noah's day indicates believers will inhabit the earth until near the close of Daniel's seventieth week.
- Sodom and Gomorrah provide a fearsome picture of the coming wrath of God upon the earth. As with Lot and his family, it seems as though believers will be persecuted where they are and then lifted away by God and His angels just before sudden destruction consumes the unbelieving world.
- Joshua's march around Jericho may provide another significant foreshadowing of believers awaiting the seventh trumpet's sound before the rapture. We may even be able to pin the rapture to occur on the Feast of Trumpets day in the Hebrew calendar! Again, I caution the reader that this is not "date setting" the Lord's return, which would be a biblical heresy.
- Paul wrote to the Corinthian believers as though they would handily know what the last trumpet was and when it would take place. This is another indication that the rapture will not be a secret and mysterious one that "leaves airplanes without pilots and automobiles without operators." The

rapture instead portends to be an earth-shattering trumpet blast accompanied by the Lord's mighty shout, in preparation for Earth's cataclysmic battle at Armageddon.

Chapter 14

Trampling Jerusalem Three and One-half Years

I was given a reed like a measuring rod and was told, "Go and measure the temple of God and the altar, and count the worshippers there. But exclude the outer court; do not measure it because it has been given to the Gentiles. They will trample on the holy city for 42 months. And I will give power to my two witnesses, and they will prophesy for 1,260 days, clothed in sackcloth."

—Revelation 11:1–3

The original temple structure, built in Jerusalem during the reign of King Solomon, was destroyed in 586 B.C. Nebuzaradan, commander of the Babylonian imperial guard, ordered the temple set on fire and the royal palace and citizens' homes of Jerusalem as well (Jeremiah 52:12–13). After the Jewish people returned from Babylonian captivity, the second temple was constructed under the leadership of Zerubbabel (Ezekiel 3:8).

Many years later, on the temple site, in 20 B.C., Herod the Great had built the equivalent of a modern fifteen-story building over the site floor of the original Holy Place and Most Holy Place. Although the impressive sanctuary was completed in eighteen months, Herod's thorough renovation of the outer courts and buildings remained incomplete until A.D. 64. The lavish second temple and its surrounding courts and structures were destroyed by fire (as with the first Solomonic temple!) by the Romans just six years later in A.D. 70.

What dates were significant in the destruction of the two temples of Jerusalem? Tish'ah B'Av, the ninth day of Av on the Hebrew ceremonial calendar, is an annual day of solemn remembrance for Jews throughout the world. On this day of the Hebrew calendar, Solomon's Temple was destroyed in 586 B.C., and 650 years later *on the same day of Tish'ah B'Av*, the elaborately renovated second Herodian temple was destroyed in A.D. 70.

For over nineteen centuries until now, the nation of Israel has been without a temple or a legitimate religious sacrifice system. Some Bible scholars claim the temple at Jerusalem will never be rebuilt, but the apostle John was told to "measure the temple and the altar and count the worshippers there (seen in John's vision)." The prophet Ezekiel also foresaw a vision of yet another temple in Jerusalem, since its measurements differ from the Solomonic temple and the second temple built by Zerubbabel, which was later expanded by Herod.

What role does the coming Antichrist play at the future temple in Jerusalem?

> "He will confirm a covenant with many for one 'seven'. In the middle of the 'seven' he will put an end to sacrifice and offering."
> Daniel 9:27a

Daniel prophesied that Antichrist would end temple sacrifices halfway through the last seven years of this age. Scripture indicates that the temple will be rebuilt in Jerusalem, and despite Christ's ending the necessity of sacrifices for temporary sin atonement (see the previous chapter), the system of sacrifices and offerings will be reinstated. Though Antichrist will proclaim inside this third temple that he is God, as in 2 Thessalonians 2:4, this act, like all things, is under the sovereignty of the true God in Heaven (Revelation 11:1). After the beast (Antichrist) and false prophet are thrown in the lake of fire, the temple will be cleansed and rededicated—holy to the Lord (Daniel 12:12).

It is my understanding that Daniel's seventieth week closes on the tenth day of the seventh month, the Day of Atonement. According to my understanding of end time events, the "confirmation of the covenant" written of by Daniel takes place seven years earlier, one day following the Hebrew Day of Atonement. What would then be the middle day of Daniel's week? The midpoint of the tribulation would thus be the tenth day of the first month, Nisan. The middle of the tribulation period falling on Nisan 10 would be significant for at least two reasons.

The 10th of Nisan was the specific day when lambs were selected for Passover slaughter by the Israelites. Nisan 10 is the date for Jesus Christ's triumphal entry into Jerusalem, commonly known as "Palm Sunday," an appropriate day indeed for the Lamb of God to be seen by those who would judge and sacrifice Him. I believe Antichrist will end the sacrificial temple system on the same day in the calendar the Paschal Lamb was selected.

The apparently fatal wound and counterfeit resurrection of Antichrist mentioned in Revelation will probably also occur on a date of great significance in the Hebrew calendar. Perhaps Antichrist will receive his "fatal" wound on the day of Passover, and his so-called "resurrection" will thus occur on the Feast of Firstfruits. The Jewish people will embrace this false Messiah until his idolatrous image is erected and he sits as a god in the temple itself. This would be when the nations "trample the outer courts" in the temple area in Jerusalem for three and one-half years while the 144,000 zealous faithful are cared for in a desert wasteland (Revelation 12:6). The events associated with the middle of the "seven" could thus occur during the first month of the Hebrew calendar if Satan is offering a specific counterfeit version of Christ's Passion Week. Look at the possible double calendar of events and see how closely Antichrist/Satan would mock the Lord Jesus Christ:

- Nisan 10: Antichrist ends temple sacrifice and offering
- Nisan 10: Christ enters Jerusalem and is worshipped
- Antichrist has received, but "rises" from, a "fatal wound"
- Christ rises from the dead
- False prophet erects image of the beast for worship (recalls Revelation 11:1 with John counting temple worshippers)
- The 144,000 (Jewish worshippers) flee beast's image and move into the desert
- Parallels the act of the disciples (Jewish followers of Christ) going into hiding after crucifixion

Should sacrifices and offerings end on the 10th of Nisan, the three-and-one-half years of gentile occupation end on the 10th of Tishri—Yom Kippur, Day of Atonement. The times of the Gentiles end, of course, with Messiah's return to redeem Israel and restore her kingdom. Remember, Antichrist has a three and one-half years of power period as granted him from ten gentile rulers (Revelation 17:12–13).

What public preaching in Jerusalem does God provide while Antichrist is mocking Christ? Others hold power at around this time—the power to preach God's Word in tremendous strength:

"And I will give power to my two witnesses, and they will prophesy for 1,260 days, clothed in sackcloth. These are the two olive trees and the two lampstands that stand before the Lord of the earth." Revelation 11:3–4

For the "two witnesses" of Revelation 11 to prophesy to the nation of Israel, they must minister in Jerusalem as promised in John's prophecy before Israel flees to the desert (Revelation 12:6). Let's continue to examine this tableau of Revelation as outlined so far in *The Last Days Calendar*:

1. The two witnesses must complete their three and one-half years of testimony (1,260 days as in Revelation 11:3 above) of necessity before the seventh/rapture trumpet sounds on Rosh HaShona, first day of the seventh month.

2. Following this scenario, since the witnesses would finish their proclamation in the sixth month of the calendar and end their preaching before the rapture, they would have *begun* preaching for three and one-half years in the twelfth month, Adar. The witnesses begin their outcry clothed in sackcloth as a sign of mourning and repentance. During the fourteenth and fifteenth days of Adar, the festival of Purim is observed, commemorating God's deliverance of the Jewish people from slaughter during the time of the Persian Empire.

As told in the book of Esther, King Xerxes, ruler of the Persian Empire, elevated one of his nobles, Haman, above the other leaders of his realm. Haman became enraged when Mordecai, a righteous Israelite, refused to kneel before Haman or pay him homage. A vengeful Haman plotted to kill not only Mordecai but also every Jewish person in the Persian Empire. In the month of Adar, sorrow turned to joy and mourning and fasting changed to celebration (see Esther 9:20–22). Queen Esther had the Jewish people in Susa join her fasting and prayer for three days. She then implored King Xerxes for deliverance from Haman on the thirteenth of Adar—a solemn remembrance known today as the Fast of Esther. Purim is first fasting and sorrow followed by days of celebration and gift giving (Esther 9:22). Compare Purim's fast and feast days with Revelation 11:

> Now when they had finished their testimony the beast that comes up from the Abyss will attack them, and overpower and kill them . . . for three and a half days men from every people, tribe, language and nation will gloat over them and will celebrate by sending each other gifts, because these two prophets had tormented those who live on the earth. Revelation 11:7–10

Do you see how the two ideas of Esther and Revelation correspond? Purim marks a time when Israel was threatened with annihilation for refusing to bow to a godless ruler from a world empire (an age-old, oft-repeated story of various tyrants trying to kill the Jewish people). Purim thus foreshadows a threatened annihilation of Israel for refusing to bow to the beast himself, Antichrist (Revelation 12:15). The other parallel, as mentioned, is "enemies killed and gifts exchanged" in Esther, with the "two witnesses killed and gifts exchanged" in Revelation 11.

The two witnesses conclude their ministry and the end of the age is imminent:

> Then they heard a loud voice from heaven saying to them, "Come up here." And they went up to heaven in a cloud, while their enemies looked on . . . The nations were angry; and your wrath has come. The time has come for judging the dead, and for rewarding your servants the prophets and your saints and those who reverence your name, both small and great—and for destroying those who live on the earth. Revelation 11:12–18

Here is a helpful Scripture chronology of the two witnesses' ministry leading to the end of the age:

1. The two witnesses are called to Heaven (Revelation 11:12)
2. A severe earthquake in Jerusalem as the seventh trumpet sounds (Revelation 11:13–15)
3. The raptured elect receive glorified bodies and their heavenly rewards (Revelation chapters 14 and 15)
4. The wedding supper of the Lamb takes place (Revelation 19:7)

Why would it logically follow that the two witnesses are received into Heaven before the rapture? (According to the pre-tribulation theory, the Church is removed and then, after the rapture, the two witnesses begin their ministry on Earth.)

There are several reasons for placing the end of the witnesses' ministry at the juncture just before the rapture. It seems as though Revelation 11 has God's wrath immediately following the witnesses' ascension and subsequent reward for believers:

> "Come up here." And they (the two witnesses) went up to heaven . . . "The time has come . . . For rewarding your servants the prophets and your saints and those who reverence your name, both small and great . . ." Revelation 11:12–18

Let's examine more closely the ministry of the witnesses before their ascension to study the future timing of these events:

> These (the witnesses) are the two olive trees and the two lampstands that stand before the Lord of the earth. If anyone tries to harm them, fire comes from their mouths and devours their enemies. This is how anyone who wants to harm them must die. These men have power to shut up the sky so that it will not rain during the time they are prophesying; and they will have power to turn the waters into blood and to strike the earth with every kind of plague as often as they want. Revelation 11:4–6

Why might God call the witnesses "olive trees"? Olive trees produce valuable fruit, highly esteemed by peoples of the Middle East. Olives are enjoyed worldwide as a nutritious food and source of oil for cooking and lamps, including the lamps for the Israelites' religious duties. Exodus 27:20 says, "Command the Israelites to bring you clear oil of pressed olives for the light so that the (temple) lamps may be kept burning."

Olives are pressed to produce oil and the oil is then filtered to screen out impurities. Clear oil is considered pure enough to fill the lamps of the sacred lampstand in the temple's Holy Place. God's people, like this pressed, fine olive oil, will become hard pressed and purified through the coming Great Tribulation. God's divine purpose to this purification? A Spirit-filled lampstand for His earthly temple, the Church.

The Lord brought the prophet Zechariah a vision regarding two olive trees, given during the restoration of Solomon's Temple. Zechariah's vision depicted two trees and one lampstand. As he sought the interpretation of the vision of two trees, the angel of the Lord replied, "These are the two who are anointed to serve the Lord of all the earth" (Zechariah 4:14).

At the time, God chose Zerubbabel from the tribe of Judah and the royal line of King David and also the current high priest, Joshua, to help restore the chosen people to the land of Israel after the Babylonian captivity to rebuild Jerusalem. All three men, the prophet Zechariah, regent Zerubbabel, and priest Joshua, foreshadowed Jesus Christ, who serves in the offices of prophet, high priest, and king for His people. Jesus is God's Word as received through the prophets (John 1:1). He is our high priest who lives to intercede for us (Hebrews 7:25) and the very King of Kings (Revelation 17:14).

The two witnesses of Revelation are anointed to serve on Earth the "Lord of the earth." They complete their ministry, and then

Jesus Christ returns to Earth to again restore Jerusalem, as in the days of Zerubbabel and Joshua. He will redeem the surviving remnant of Israel, as when a remnant returned from the Babylonian captivity. Jesus will then establish His throne in God's temple at Jerusalem.

Who exactly are the two witnesses; may they be identified clearly at this time through Scripture? The two witnesses are empowered to "shut up the sky" so rain will not reach the earth. The prophet Elijah brought divine judgment to Israel during the reign of the evil King Ahab (see 1 Kings 16:30), including a three-year drought, until the judgment of Ahab's prophets of Baal (see 1 Kings 18:45). Many theologians agree that Elijah, taken to Heaven still alive, will be one of the two witnesses to bring a great drought.

Malachi 4:5 speaks of the "forerunner" of Jesus, John the Baptist, and may also refer to Elijah's return at the end of the age as one of the two witnesses of Revelation 11.

> "See, I will send you the prophet Elijah before that great and dreadful day of the LORD comes." Malachi 4:5

What of the second witness? Some believe it is Enoch who did not die but was "raptured" to Heaven, like Elijah, in a fiery whirlwind (see Genesis 5:24). Strong evidence, however, points to Moses, not Enoch, as the second witness joining Elijah. Like Moses, the witnesses have power to change water to blood and to bring great plagues to Earth.

Moses is the archetypal Bible figure representing the law of God, while Elijah represents God's chosen prophets. Both Elijah and Moses were with Jesus Christ at His transfiguration (Matthew 17:3). Jude 9 explains that the archangel Michael disputed with Satan over the deceased body of Moses—perhaps knowing Moses' ministry was left uncompleted. (Moses was to bring His people to

Israel yet died outside of Israel.) Thus, Moses gets to see the Promised Land for himself, and Elijah finishes his preaching in Jerusalem. (Elijah was to prophesy in Jerusalem but was taken away by God after he fled from Jezebel to Mount Sinai.)

One argument proffered against Moses as one of the witnesses is found in an application of Hebrews 9:27, which reads, "Just as man is destined to die once, and after that to face judgment . . .", indicating that Moses' death rules out the possibility of his return as a living witness. Jesus Christ, however, is the resurrection and the life (John 11:25). Lazarus and Jairus' daughter were raised from death by Jesus. With God all things are possible—in accordance with His Word, of course! Moses and Elijah appearing alive at the transfiguration of Jesus would prefigure this prophetic possibility of their dramatic return to Earth.

No matter who the two witnesses are, they will be anointed to fulfill God's divine plan. Those preferring to reject Christ to walk in darkness will be tormented by the light of the two lampstands. (See John 3:9 and confer with Revelation 11:10.) My hope and prayer is that many others will understand their witness and gratefully receive their powerful and dramatic testimony.

Summary of Chapter Fourteen

- God's temple at Jerusalem was destroyed two times on the same day of the Hebrew calendar—the 9th of Av.
- There will be a third temple in Jerusalem, and Antichrist will end sacrifices here. As with the temple desecration caused by Antiochus Epiphanes in the Chanukah story, the temple will again receive a great abomination on the altar—this time the beast himself!
- If the midpoint of the tribulation occurs on the 10th of Nisan, Antichrist, in his "death and resurrection," will more

perfectly mock Christ's death and resurrection, which began on the 10th of Nisan, nearly two millennia ago.

- The "two witnesses" preach powerfully for three and one-half years in the city where Antichrist mocks Christ—Jerusalem. If Christ raptures His Church at the Jewish New Year, Antichrist "dies and rises" over Passover and Firstfruits, and the two witnesses complete three and one-half years of testimony just before the seventh trumpet sounds, the witnesses' preaching would have begun on the fourteenth day of Adar, when Purim is observed (commemorating God's deliverance of the Jewish people from an evil empire).

- The two witnesses are so closely aligned with Moses and Elijah that many commentators believe these two mighty prophets will personally return as God's two lampstands for the end of this age. The two witnesses also parallel the ministry of Joshua (Temple High Priest), Zechariah, Zerubbabel, and the Lord Jesus, who helped increase the zeal of God's people and cleanse and rededicate God's temple to prepare the way of Christ.

- Continuing on our tribulation scenario as outlined in the last several chapters, the second half of Daniel's "seven," the last three and one-half years of the seven years of tribulation, will be marked by persecution of God's saints and the testimony of the two witnesses. At the sounding of the seventh trumpet of Revelation, the Church is raptured and God's bowls of wrath are poured upon the earth and its inhabitants. Ten days after, Jesus will triumphantly return to Earth as conquering King to mete out punishment to His enemies, redeem Israel, and establish His throne on Earth. The next chapter highlights Christ's future fulfillment of the Jubilee and Feast of Tabernacles.

Chapter 15

Why Is There a Special Blessing for Waiting 1,335 Days?

"From the time the daily sacrifice is abolished and the abomination that causes desolation is set up, there will be 1,290 days. Blessed is the one who waits for and reaches the end of the 1,335 days."

—Daniel 12:11–12

D aniel 12 reveals that a period of three and one-half years will elapse in which Israel's great distress and final deliverance will be accomplished (Daniel 12:1–7). If my understanding is correct and the daily sacrifice is abolished on the tenth day of Nisan, 1,260 days later brings us the Day of Atonement, observed on the tenth day of Tishri. This chapter will explore what the Scriptures might be telling us about the remaining seventy-five-day period.

We have two significant time periods in Daniel 12:11–12, which extend past the time of the return of Christ to the earth. The first is 1,290 days, counted from the day daily sacrifice in the temple is abolished, that is, thirty days after the 1,260 days (three and one-half years). This thirty-day month, added to the 1,260 days, brings us from Nisan 10 to the tenth day of the eighth month, Heshvan, which falls thirty days after the Day of Atonement.

So what might the thirty-day period between the 1,260th day and 1,290th day imply?

> And when the whole community learned that Aaron had died, *the entire house of Israel mourned* for him for thirty days. Numbers 20:29

> On that day the weeping in Jerusalem will be great, like the weeping of Hadad Rimmon in the plain of Megiddo. The land will mourn, each clan by itself, with their wives by themselves . . . Zechariah 12:11–12a

> The Israelites grieved for Moses in the plains of Moab for thirty days, until the time of weeping and mourning was over. Deuteronomy 34:8

> Look, he is coming with the clouds, and every eye will see him, even those who pierced him; and all the peoples of the earth will mourn because of him. So shall it be! Amen. Revelation 1:7

When Israel's first high priest, Aaron, died, the entire nation mourned him for thirty days. When Moses the deliverer died, there was again great weeping and mourning for thirty days. On the day of the rapture, the Lord comes with the clouds (souls of those who died in Christ) and there is mourning, and Israel will grieve bitterly for their Messiah whom they have pierced.

Unlike the people of the gentile nations, who will not repent of their immorality (Revelation 9:21), Israel will come to mourn in such a way that, as individuals change their minds regarding Christ, salvation is ushered in (see Romans 11:25–26; 2 Corinthians 7:10). When the Lord returns to the earth to redeem Israel, the great weeping and mourning will be like the sorrow for righteous

King Josiah after Pharaoh's archers mortally wounded him in battle on the plain of Megiddo. (See 2 Chronicles 35:20–27; this is the place where Armageddon will be fought!)

I believe the nation will grieve and mourn for Christ, the "One they have pierced," for a thirty-day period, beginning 1,260 days after sacrifices and offerings are abolished by Antichrist. This follows the story pattern of Zechariah 12.

What does "Armageddon" mean? "Armageddon, is taken from a Greek word, actually a translation of the Hebrew *Har-Megiddo* meaning, "Mount Megiddo." An ancient city called Megiddo has been unearthed by archaeologists. This city was located in the mountains of northern Israel, across the Plain of *Esdraelon* from Nazareth. *Esdraelon* is another form of the Hebrew *Jezreel*, meaning "God has sown." In the final battle of this age, the nations who have "sown to the wind" will reap the whirlwind of God's outpoured wrath.

> Then they gathered the kings together to the place that in Hebrew is called Armageddon . . . I saw the beast and the kings of the earth and their armies gathered together to make war against the rider on the horse and his army. Revelation 16:16; 19:19

The Lord Jesus Christ will return to Earth riding a white horse. The armies of Heaven will follow, riding white horses and dressed in fine linen. His eyes ablaze, the Son of God will tread the press of God's fury, striking the nations with the sword of His mouth. He will rule them for one millennium with an iron scepter (Psalm 2; Revelation 19:11–15). Jesus will rule from Jerusalem on God's holy hill (Psalm 2:6).

And what of the remaining forty-five-day period? What is the 1,335th day? The Lord declared to King David that Messiah would issue from David's line and that Messiah's kingdom would be established eternally (2 Samuel 7:13–16). Before Jesus takes His rightful place on His throne in Jerusalem, His temple must be sanctified and rededicated to Him. I believe the temple cleansing will be completed as the 1,335 days of Daniel 12 are completed.

For our review, the Hebrew calendar consists of months that are thirty days in length. The 1,290 days would be completed three and one-half years plus one month after the midpoint of the seven-year tribulation period. The 1,335 days are completed forty-five days after the 1,290 days end (1,335 days - 1,290 days = 45 days). If the 1,290-day period ends on the seventh day of Heshvan, the twenty-fifth day of the ninth month, Kislev, is the 1,335th day. Any Jewish person surviving the tribulation and after will be extremely blessed to reach the end of 1,335 days—the Feast of Dedication (Chanukah)! This commemoration is also known as the Festival of Lights (of God, the Light of the world) and is a time of cleansing for the temple in Jerusalem.

Again, as a chronology, we would have:

1. One thousand two-hundred-sixty days are complete and tribulation's last three and one-half years are ended on Yom Kippur, Day of Atonement
2. Israel mourns her dead, her rejection of Messiah, and the world's tribulations for thirty days, as they mourned Aaron and Moses for thirty-day periods
3. Forty-five days of judgments, ceremonies, and celebrations end as Jesus cleanses His temple, which has been defiled by Antichrist, by His own glory—and it is seventy-five days completed in total from Day of Atonement to Chanukah, festival of the lamplight and cleansing of the temple!

What elements of the Chanukah story parallel the events of Revelation as prophesied by Daniel?

Following the death of Alexander the Great, his empire was divided four ways with Seleucus ruling Syria. Antiochus IV was a cruel tyrant who came to the Seleucid throne in Syria. He led a vicious campaign against Jerusalem, claiming to be a god and calling himself Antiochus Epiphanes (an epiphany is "God manifest" or "visibly a god"). Antiochus defiled the temple by erecting an idol of Zeus there—bearing Antiochus' own image to boot! (Sound familiar?) He further polluted the Holy of Holies by slaughtering a pig (an unclean [non-kosher] animal) upon the temple altar.

After three years of guerrilla warfare led by the Maccabees, the Jewish people were partially liberated from Antiochus and Syrian occupation. Apocryphal literature records that the holy altar was rebuilt on the twenty-fifth of Kislev in 165 B.C., exactly three years to the day from its defilement by Antiochus. According to Jewish tradition, the Maccabees found only one cruse of unpolluted oil useful for fueling the temple's golden lampstand and only enough oil inside the cruse for one day's light. Miraculously, says the Chanukah story, the oil burned brightly for eight days until a new supply of oil could be brought from a distance, consecrated, and put in service.

We know from John's gospel that Jesus went up to the temple in Jerusalem during the Feast of Dedication (Chanukah) indeed declaring throughout John's record that He is the Light of the world (see John chapter 10; also John 1:4, 9; 3:19; 8:12; 9:5; 12:46). We also can see obvious parallels between the evil ruler Antiochus IV and Antichrist.

I believe that as the second temple was cleansed and rededicated to the Lord on Kislev 25, so shall the third temple, defiled by the filth of Antichrist, be cleansed and rededicated on the twenty-fifth day of Kislev. The Lord Jesus will again go to the temple during the Feast of Dedication. This time, God's Son will take His rightful place upon the throne in the Holy of Holies.

"Then have the trumpet sounded everywhere on the tenth day of the seventh month; on the Day of Atonement sound the trum-

pet throughout your land. Consecrate the fiftieth year and proclaim liberty throughout the land to all its inhabitants. It shall be
a jubilee for you; each one of you is to return to his family property and each to his own clan." Leviticus 25: 9–10

The thirty-day period of mourning and the rededication of the
temple take place following the Day of Atonement and the return
of Christ. The Day of Atonement is the scriptural day when all the
sins of the nation of Israel are put aside. We are looking at total
restoration of the people of Israel to their Land of Promise, as in
Leviticus 25. Note in 25:9–10 that the Day of Atonement repentance was tied intimately to annunciating the jubilee year of restoration and glory to Israel.

What about today in modern times? What is the status of modern Israel? Is modern Israel found in ancient biblical prophecy?

On May 14, 1948, following more than 2,500 years of struggle,
holocausts and inquisitions, and a United Nations proclamation
on behalf of the peoples of the world, outcasts of Israel gathered
from Diaspora formed an independent Jewish nation.

"Then you, my people, will know that I am the LORD, when I
open your graves and bring you up from them. I will put my
Spirit in you and you will live, and I will settle you in your own
land. Then you will know that I the LORD have spoken, and I
have done it, declares the LORD." Ezekiel 37:13–14

The prophet Ezekiel was taken by God's Spirit and set in the
middle of a great valley. The valley was filled with dry bones and
Ezekiel was commanded to prophesy over these remains. God
promised to attach tendons to the bones and make flesh come
upon them as their covering. The Lord promised that, later, He
would put His living breath in them and they would arise to life
(Ezekiel 37:1–6).

Anyone viewing films about the European Holocaust with its mass graves of Jewish victims has seen valleys literally filled from dry bones. Ezekiel's vision symbolizes the whole house of Israel (dry bones) scattered throughout the nations of the world (graves in Diaspora). The Lord promised to gather His chosen people and bring them again into Israel. Following the murder of six million Jews, the "dry bones" were more completely joined together—in less than three years' time—to become a sovereign nation.

Dry bones are dry for a number of reasons. One of note: because apart from the body they are not surrounded with blood (without the shedding of blood there cannot be atonement for sin [Hebrews 9:22]). Israel has gathered as a nation without a temple or altar for their use. At first the nation did not even possess the holy city of Jerusalem. It would take nearly twenty years and three astounding wars before Israel reclaimed inner Jerusalem, the City of David.

Israel's miraculous victory in the Six-Day War placed Jerusalem back under Jewish control. After the bones of Ezekiel are covered with flesh, muscle, and skin, the Lord will put His breath (Holy Spirit) in them. Although the nation has already celebrated its fiftieth anniversary, it was not a biblical jubilee (fiftieth anniversary celebration) in fullest possible sense. Israel will not come to full spiritual life until each individual accepts the One that they have pierced, as promised. When Christ returns, I believe that, following the great mourning on Yom Kippur, liberty through the true Christ will be proclaimed throughout the land.

How was the ancient jubilee to be fulfilled in Jesus Christ? What happens to Israel during the future jubilee?

"The Spirit of the Lord is on me, because he has anointed me to preach good news to the poor. He has sent me to proclaim freedom for the prisoners and recovery of sight for the blind, to re-

lease the oppressed, to proclaim the year of the Lord's favor."
Luke 4:18–19

After being tempted in the wilderness, Jesus returned to the
Galilee area. On a Sabbath day, Jesus went to the synagogue in
Nazareth and was honored by being called upon to read from the
scroll of Isaiah, the liturgical reading for that Saturday. After reading from Isaiah 61:1–2, Jesus startled the congregation with the
text of His message, expounding on the passage with the incredible "Today this scripture is fulfilled in your hearing." (See Luke
4:20–21.)

Jesus' Messiahship and mission was to preach good news of
salvation and proclaim God's favor to Israel. "The year of the Lord's
favor" refers to the biblical Year of Jubilee, a semi-centennial celebration declared every fifty years. Jubilee was to be a time of
liberation and freedom when slaves were freed, debts were can-
celed, and ancestral property was returned to its rightful heirs.

> "In this Year of Jubilee everyone is to return to His own prop-
> erty . . . Land must not be sold permanently, because the land
> is mine . . ." Leviticus 25:13; 23a

Today the state of Israel is constantly coerced by the nations of
the world to trade land for peace. The day Israel declared her in-
dependence she was invaded by five enemy nations avowed to
drive the chosen people off Palestinian land and into the Mediter-
ranean Sea. For nineteen years, for one example, Syria continu-
ously used Golan as a staging area to drop bombs upon Israeli
farms beneath the heights. In 1967, one result of the astounding
victory in the Six-Day War was Israel's regaining the biblical territories of Judea and Samaria through reconquest of Golan. Many
worldwide are the claims that the occupied territories must be
given away for a mere promise of peace. Others realize this land is

not technically Israel's to trade since it belongs to the Lord under His sovereign protection!

Israel is continually in jeopardy with potential attack from enemies outside her borders and potential Israeli victims ravaged by wanton terrorism within. The nation and the world, weary of struggle, yearn for lasting peace in the Middle East. When Antichrist arises on the scene to broker a confirmation of a peace agreement for the Middle East, Israel will eagerly embrace his confirmation of an existing seven-year covenant.

The appeasement of mortal enemies vowed to annihilate Israel is, biblically speaking, unattainable and foolhardy without Christ's direct intervention. The false Messiah, Antichrist, can only usher a false peace, a bow without arrow, incredibly deadly in its deception. The only lasting peace for Israel will come when Yeshua/Jesus, the Prince of Peace, returns as conquering king of the nations and Israel's "kinsman redeemer":

> "If an alien or temporary resident living among you becomes rich and one of your countrymen becomes poor and sells himself to the alien living among you or a member of the alien's clan, he retains the right of redemption after he has sold himself. One of His relatives may redeem him." Leviticus 25:47–48

The glorious 1000–year millennium is the topic of our next chapter.

Summary of Chapter Fifteen

- Daniel 12 mentions two significant dates: 1,290 days and 1,335 days after the midpoint of the tribulation. Scholars still debate the significance of these periods. On our timeline, 1,290 days gives us thirty days following the Day of Atonement, thirty days being in Scripture an especially grievous mourning period for Israel. If the tribulation ends on the Day of Atonement, the 1,335th day is to be the biblical Feast of Dedication, or Chanukah, the festival of the Light of the world and the time for rededicating God's temple!

- The traditional stories and secular histories surrounding the figure of Antiochus IV of Syria give further indication that Chanukah is a picture of a great Chanukah to come. Israel awaits the coming return of Jesus Christ to His cleansed and rededicated temple in Jerusalem—cleansed of the filth and idolatry of Antichrist—following the tribulation period of God's judgment.

- Israel is a unique nation in history, formed in one day, two separate times—following the Exodus from Egypt and also the proclamation of the United Nations in 1948. Ezekiel foresaw a secular Jewish nation awaiting God's Spirit-led revival in the end of days. Always at war with her neighbors, trading Israeli land for peace may become Antichrist's bright idea, but the covenant he will confirm between Abraham's warring children is doomed solely to misery and failure for God's people.

- Jesus inaugurated one aspect of His ministry by declaring He is the fulfillment of Isaiah's prophecy of Messiah delivering and leading His Jewish people. He awaits the fulfillment of the latter half of Isaiah 61:2, judgment for the nations of the world and for Israel. He will afterward deliver Israel into a glorious jubilee of redemption and liberation.

- Jesus is the Lion from the tribe of Judah, a natural relative through David to the House of Israel. The year of the Lord's favor, the Jubilee, is a special time when those of Israel sold as slaves could be redeemed—liberated for a price— by a relative. There is an analogy with unsaved Israelites in spiritual bondage and enslaved to sin. Jesus purchased men for God with His atoning blood for Israel and for every nation (Revelation 5:9). After the rapture of the church on Rosh HaShona, could Jesus return on the Day of Atonement and proclaim the Year of Jubilee?

Chapter 16

Noah had Forty Days' Rain, but Believers "Reign" for 1,000 Years

I saw thrones on which were seated those who had been given authority to judge. And I saw the souls of those who had been beheaded because of their testimony for Jesus and because of the word of God. They had not worshipped the beast or His image and had not received His mark on their foreheads or their hands. They came to life and reigned with Christ a thousand years.

—Revelation 20:4

The word *millennium* is derived from compounding two Latin terms, *mille* (thousand) and *annus* (year). The premillennial view of the end of the age is a doctrine affirming the triumphant return of Christ to Earth before He establishes a literal thousand-year kingdom. There are Christians who hold instead to a non-literal, or symbolic, interpretation of Revelation 20. Their position, "amillennialism," means "without one thousand years." They interpret the one thousand years of Revelation 20:4 as a metaphor representing a prophecy of a long but indeterminate time.

Does the amillennial view of the Bible (no thousand-year reign of Christ) hold true? Amillennialists theorize that Revelation's millennium portrays the present church age and the believers who have died in Christ rule alongside Him presently in Heaven. This view discounts the fact that the Scriptures speak of one thousand years as a time period commencing *after* the resurrection of the righteous, including believers martyred during the reign of Antichrist (see Revelation 20:5–6).

During the millennium, Satan is bound and locked in the Abyss for one thousand years' time (Revelation 20:3). During this present age, however, Christians are admonished to be prepared since Satan prowls for their harm like a roaring lion (1 Peter 5:8). The Church is urged to submit to God at this time and resist Satan (James 4:7). If Satan were bound already, that is, if the millennium were today's church age, we would not need God's armor, given to withstand Satan's schemes (see Ephesians 6:11).

Is there more evidence indicating a literal millennium? Jesus said of His kingdom:

> "My kingdom is not of this world. If it were, my servants would fight to prevent my arrest by the Jews. But now my kingdom is from another place." John 18:36

Jesus Christ affirmed to Pontius Pilate that His kingdom is not of Earth but from another place (Heaven). One underlying meaning of this remark is that in the future, Christ's kingdom will established on Earth from "the top down," that is, from Heaven's direct intercession.

What millennial view does God working "top down" contraindicate? The understanding that God will establish His own kingdom stands in contradiction to many who believe the world will eventually be "Christianized," resulting in a theocratic period of peace before Christ's return. These postmillennialists (or "after one thousand years") seems to omit Christ's dire prediction that many will turn from the faith, betraying and hating each other before His amazing return (see Matthew 24:10; Mark 13:12–13).

In contrast, the premillennial view allows for both a literal and spiritual fulfillment of prophesied events. This concept, the literal return of Christ before the end of the church age, was commonplace among Jesus' disciples! After Jesus predicted that the temple would be thrown down so utterly that every stone would be separated from every other, He left the temple and went to the Mount of Olives. As He rested there, the disciples approached Him, asking:

> "Tell us . . .when will this [destruction of the temple] happen, and what will be the sign of your coming [return] and of the end of the [church/judgment of Israel] age?" Matthew 24:3

The disciples anticipated: 1) the destruction of the temple, 2) followed by the return of Christ ("what will be the sign of your coming") and then, 3) the end of the age. Jesus replied to their question, not speaking of world peace before His return. Rather, He told of warfare, endemic famine, and violent earthquakes as the beginning of birth pains. Jesus did not foretell a Christianized world but great persecution and hatred of the saints by all nations (Matthew 24:6–9). Judgment was also to fall on the House of Israel before its millennial restoration:

> Peter answered him, "We have left everything to follow you! What then will there be for us?" Jesus said to them, "I tell you the truth, at the renewal of all things, when the Son of Man sits on His glorious throne, you who have followed me will sit on twelve thrones, judging the twelve tribes of Israel." Matthew 19:27–28

Although the primary intent of the book of Revelation is to reveal future events that must of necessity occur (Revelation 1:1),

John envisioned thrones on which were seated those already given authority in judgment (Revelation 4:4) before the bulk of Revelation's events unfolded. John saw future fulfillment of a past promise of reward given by Jesus to the original apostles who had left everything to follow Him (Matthew 19:27).

[Author's note: Many Christians have trouble deciphering Judas' role among the apostles. Judas Iscariot was a thief of funds marked to help the poor (John 12:6). He betrayed Christ and was traitorous (Luke 6:16; John 18:5). Although Judas was remorseful for the betrayal of Christ, he did not seek God's forgiving grace but hanged himself (Matthew 27:4). Judas will not be a part of the resurrection of the righteous at the renewal of all things. Instead it seems likely that Paul, an apostle of Christ Jesus by the command of God (1 Timothy 1:1), will be the twelfth enthroned with the eleven disciples to judge the tribes of Israel. God, of course, in His sovereignty, can have other elders sit with Him in judgment and will indeed have Christians to help Him judge (see 1 Corinthians 6:3; Revelation 4:4).]

What type of exciting things will occur with the 144,000 during the millennium? The 144,000 Israelites of Revelation 7 are the firstfruits of God and comprised of 12,000 from each of the tribes of Israel (Revelation 7:4; 14:4). The Israelite tribe of Dan is unlisted in the account of the tribes in Revelation 7:5–8. The tribe of Dan indulged in idolatry from soon after first settling their land until the Assyrian captivity of the Northern Kingdom (see Judges 18:30). Dan will not share in the privilege and honor afforded the 144,000 who will make up the unique entourage of the Lamb (Revelation 14:4). The Danites will, however, be afforded their ancestral land share during the millennium.

Further, the 144,000 are not part of the rapture when the elect gather and meet Christ in the air. Instead, they are redeemed from the earth (Revelation 14:3). It seems as though the surviving remnant of Israel will enter the thousand-year reign of Christ in mortal, corruptible bodies. The twelve tribes will dwell in the Promised Land as God has apportioned it to them (see Ezekiel 48).

Who will rule over the millennial Israelites? Israel, reestablished as a theocracy, will have Jesus Christ Himself as the supreme civil governing authority. In contrast, the elect believers who are raptured will resurrect to life in immortal, incorruptible bodies to rule and reign with Christ (Revelation 20:4). Christ will reign visibly and supremely over mankind:

> The LORD will be king over the whole earth. On that day there will be one LORD, and His name the only name. Zechariah 14:9

The history of our fallen world is marked by evil despots, who ruled vast empires from their capitals. During the millennium, Christ will rule from Jerusalem, in righteousness, with a rod of iron (Psalm 2:8–12)!

> The LORD says to my Lord: "Sit at my right hand until I make your enemies a footstool for your feet." The LORD will extend your mighty scepter from Zion; you will rule in the midst of your enemies. Psalm 110:1–2

After Jesus offered Himself on the cross, the sacrifice for sin, He sat at the right hand of God in power (Hebrews 10:12). When Christ returns to Earth as conquering king, He will reign with full power and authority over His enemies. Survivors from the nations will enter the millennium in natural, corruptible bodies. Although the armies of the nations will be destroyed in the winepress of God's fury (see Revelation 19:18), persons who have taken the mark of the beast and survived the tribulation, I believe, will remain alive until the coming of Christ. Their destiny is grim, but they will offer oblation to the Lord:

> Then the survivors from all the nations that have attacked Jerusalem will go up year after year to worship the King, the LORD Almighty, and to celebrate the Feast of Tabernacles. Zechariah 14:16

So, what happens following the millennium? The return of Christ to Earth will usher in a renewal of all things in the cosmos (Matthew 19:28). Through Jesus Christ all created things were installed (Colossians 1:16), and His original creation was extremely good in nature (Genesis 1:31). The "renewal of all things" has creation restored to an Eden-ic state of being good. I believe Christians need to make the distinction between the creation being restored during the millennium and the perfection of the new Eden, the eternal kingdom, that follows final judgment, *after* the millennium.

Christ reigns in the midst of His enemies during the millennium. But when the thousand years end, all whose names are blotted from the book of life are cast into eternal fire (Revelation 20:15). During the millennium, survivors from all nations are called annually to Jerusalem to worship the King (Zechariah 14:16). But during the time of the coming eternal kingdom, only people whose names are written in the book of life may enter into the holy, heavenly city (see Revelation 21:27). The righteous may look to the promise of a new heaven and a new earth (2 Peter 3:13; Revelation 21:1).

What will happen on Earth during the millennium? During the millennium, both the just and the unjust will live on a tribulation-scarred earth that has then been gloriously renewed.

Originally, man had dominion over all the earth, including the animal kingdom (Genesis 1:28). When Adam willfully disobeyed God, sin entered the world and death through sin (Romans 5:12). Due to man's disobedience the earth was also cursed (Genesis 3:17) when Adam and Eve chose to obey Satan instead of obeying God.

Don't you know that when you offer yourselves to someone to obey him as slaves, you are slaves to the one whom you obey— whether you are slaves to sin, which leads to death, or to obedience, which leads to righteousness? Romans 6:16

Man's dominion was handed to Satan who became the "prince of this world" (John 12:31). Sin's power became our master. What was very good, the creation, became corrupt, and the world was placed under the control of the devil (1 John 5:19). Satan could tempt Jesus in the wilderness by offering Him the kingdoms of Earth because they were his to grant (Matthew 4:8–9).

But the gift (of salvation) is not like the trespass (of fallen Adam's sin). For if the many died by the trespass of one man, (Adam) how much more did God's grace and the gift that came by the grace of the one man, Jesus Christ, overflow to the many! Romans 5:15

Through Christ's death on the cross and His resurrection from the dead, the Son of Man has defeated Satan. All authority in Heaven and Earth has been given to Jesus Christ (Matthew 28:18). The first Adam lost dominion through sin. The last Adam, Jesus (1 Corinthians 15:45), regained dominion by His perfect, sinless sacrifice. During the millennium, Satan will be bound, locked away from deceiving the nations for a millennium (Revelation 20:2–3). Warfare will cease for this time. Satan, prince of this world, will be bound, awaiting a brief release before his eternal judgment, while the Prince of Peace will justly judge between the nations.

He will judge between the nations and settle disputes for many peoples. They will beat their swords into plowshares and their spears into pruning hooks. Nation will not take up sword against nation, nor will they train for war anymore. Isaiah 2:4

There will be a restoration of Earth itself to the state existing before the curse of Eden. Jerusalem will be like the Garden of Eden. Remember John the Baptist? He proclaimed that he was a voice calling in the desert and preaching a baptism of repentance for the forgiveness of sins (Matthew 3:1–2; Mark 1:1–4; Luke 3:3–6). John quoted from the prophecy stating that every valley shall be filled in, every mountain and hill lowered, and man will see God's salvation (Isaiah 40:3–5). The coming millennial kingdom is a fulfillment of this prophecy.

When the seventh Revelation angel pours his bowl into the air, an earthquake so severe will bash the earth so that cities worldwide will collapse and every mountain and island will be moved from its location (Revelation 6:14; 16:17–20). Jesus will establish His glorious throne atop Mount Zion as Isaiah's prophecy is literally fulfilled, while all men see God's salvation, Jesus:

> They were looking intently up into the sky as he was going, when suddenly two men dressed in white stood beside them. "Men of Galilee," they said, "why do you stand here looking up into the sky? This same Jesus, who has been taken from you into heaven, will come back in the same way you have seen him go into heaven." Acts 1:10–11

> Then the LORD will go out and fight against those nations, as he fights in the day of battle. On that day His feet will stand on the Mount of Olives, east of Jerusalem, and the Mount of Olives will be split in two from east to west, forming a great valley, with half the mountain moving north and half moving south. Zechariah 14:3–4

Just before the ascension of Christ to Heaven, Jesus and the disciples were in the vicinity of Bethany, on the Mount of Olives (Luke 24:50–51). While the Lord blessed His disciples, He was taken before their eyes as a cloud hid Him from their sight (Acts 1:9). As their gaze was fixed skyward, the Lord rose higher—until only the soles of His feet were visible before He finally disappeared from their view:

> Look, there on the mountains, the feet of the one who brings good news, who proclaims peace! Nahum 1:15a

Jesus, resurrected and glorified, will descend from Heaven, and the blessed feet of the Son of Man will again stand on the Mount of Olives. He will bring the good news of salvation to Israel and proclaim a millennium era of unprecedented peace for the world. The mile-long ridge known as the Mount of Olives will no longer overlook the temple mount but will split into two halves, forming a great valley:

> In the last days the mountain of the LORD's temple will be established as chief among the mountains; it will be raised above the hills, and all nations will stream to it. Isaiah 2:2

> But Jerusalem will be raised up and remain in its place . . . Zechariah 14:10b

What happens at the third temple following Antichrist's rule or terror? All the lands of Judah surrounding the holy city will be leveled, but Jerusalem will be lifted in its foundation. Six hundred years before the birth of Christ, Ezekiel cried out to God and said:

> "Ah, Sovereign LORD! Are you going to destroy the entire remnant of Israel in this outpouring of your [final] wrath on Jerusalem?" Ezekiel 9:8

The sin of the chosen people was exceedingly great at the time of Ezekiel. The land was full of bloodshed, and Jerusalem was replete with injustice. Idols were worshipped inside God's temple. These abominations resulted in the visible divine presence's departing the holy city. The Shekinah glory, God's presence to His people, rose from above the ark and between the cherubim in the most holy place, moving to the threshold of the temple (Ezekiel 10:4). Then the glory presence stopped at the east gate of the temple (Ezekiel 10:19). Finally the glory of the Lord went from within Jerusalem, stopping at the Mount of Olives (Ezekiel 10:23).

When Christ returns, He will renew all things, including the restoration of His visible divine presence in the temple. The glorified Son of Man will sit on His throne in heavenly glory (Matthew 25:31). Jesus will return from Heaven by descending to the Mount of Olives, and reversing the movement of the glory in Ezekiel 10, He will enter the east gate, process to the threshold of the temple, enter the Holy of Holies, and sit on His glorious throne.

According to Ezekiel's vision, structures and furnishings of the first and second temples are not mentioned as part of the third temple. Important omissions in the third temple include:

- No "bronzed sea" with water for ritual cleansing of the temple priests. The Israelite priesthood was of necessity concerned with external ceremony. Believers today are a holy nation and royal priesthood (1 Peter 2:9), washed inwardly instead by the water of the living Word (Ephesians 5:26; Hebrews 10:22).
- No wall dividing the outer court, frequented by Gentiles, from the inner temple area. (Christ destroyed the dividing wall of hostility by abolishing in His flesh the law with its many commandments and regulations—Ephesians 2:14–15.)
- There will be no need of a lampstand because the glory of God Himself will light the temple (Revelation 21:23).

- No veiled curtain separates the Holy Place from the Most Holy Place. (The curtain was torn in two when Christ died on the cross—Luke 23:45.)
- Instead of the Ark of the Covenant, where God's glory hovered over the mercy seat, Christ will be seated on His throne (Matthew 19:28; 25:31). A new and living way into the Holy of Holies was opened for us through Christ's body (Hebrews 10:19–20).
- There will be no altar of incense. The smoke of the incense was to conceal the atonement cover above the covenant ark so that the high priest would not die from the sight of God's glory (see Leviticus 16:13). During the millennium, the glory of the Lord will be unconcealed, for we will see Him face to face (see 1 Corinthians 13:12).

During the coming millennium, the territory of Israel will approximate the borders of the nation at the time of David and Solomon (Ezekiel 47:15–20), excluding the Transjordan (the Transjordan was never within the boundaries of the Promised Land). The mountain of the Lord will be the highest point on Earth (Isaiah 2:2). The twelve tribes will be restored to dwell in their ancestral territories (Ezekiel 48:1–29) and stand as judged by Christ's disciples (Matthew 19:28). Christ will rule His enemies with power and authority from His throne in Zion (Psalm 2:8–9; Psalm 110:1–2). Glorified saints will reign with Christ for one thousand years (2 Timothy 2:12; Revelation 20:4).

Two classes of people, I believe, will enter the millennium in mortal bodies. Jewish unbelievers surviving the tribulation will be saved as Christ returns but are not part of the glorified, raptured church. They will dwell in natural bodies. Gentile unbelievers surviving the tribulation will dwell in peace in their own lands. They too, will have corruptible, mortal bodies. People will live and die, raising families of descendants, during the millennial reign of Christ on Earth. Those dwelling in Jerusalem will live an increased life span, as did the patriarchs who lived before the flood of Noah's day:

> Never again will there be in it an infant who lives but a few days, or an old man who does not live out His years; he who dies at a hundred will be thought a mere youth; he who fails to reach a hundred will be considered accursed. Isaiah 65:20

Jerusalem will be Eden restored. It will be as Paradise was before its corruption through sin. Note that there will be people considered cursed since they failed to live at least one hundred years! There may be children born in Israel from believing parents who reject Christ as Savior or the very rare child who dies in youth (and faith). During the millennium, there may also be children born from unbelieving gentile parents. Their parents are headed for a lost eternity, and they received the beast's mark. There may be Gentiles born during the millennium, and some of their names may be untarnished in the book of life (Revelation 20:15).

> "The wolf and the lamb will feed together, and the lion will eat straw like the ox, but dust will be the serpent's food. They will neither harm nor destroy on all my holy mountain," says the LORD. Isaiah 65:25

On Mount Zion, even the most ferocious and dangerous beasts will become docile and no longer carnivorous. In Eden, each seed-bearing plant and fruit-bearing tree was given as food (Genesis 1:29). Man did not eat meat until after the Noahic flood (Genesis 9:3). A pastoral lifestyle will be reinstated on God's holy mountain. The old serpent, Satan, however, will still be accursed:

"For dust you are and to dust you will return." Genesis 3:19b

Dust symbolizes death. The serpent still eats dust—there is no redemption given in Scripture for fallen angels. The devil will be bound for a thousand years and kept from deceiving the nations (Revelation 20:2–3). After the millennium, Satan will be released briefly to provoke a final assault against God's people. The enemies of God will be devoured by heavenly fire. Then the great deceiver will be thrown into the lake of burning sulfur where he will suffer eternal torment (Revelation 20:7–10).

The wicked dead of the ages and any unbelievers who died during the millennium will be raised to life, to stand before a great throne for judgment according to their works in life—a judgment none can stand (Psalm 130:3). The Christian has already been judged for reward—this is a great judgment as to degree of punishment (see Luke 12:47–48). Those with names blotted from God's book of life will be cast into a fiery lake.

The coming fulfillment of the Feast of Tabernacles and its relation to the millennium will be discussed at length in the next chapter.

Summary of Chapter Sixteen

- Christians hold three disparate views regarding the one thousand-year period mentioned in Revelation 20:

  1. Amillennialists theorize that Revelation's millennium portrays the present church age—this view discounts the fact that the one thousand years commence *after* the resurrection of the righteous, including believers martyred during the reign of Antichrist. (See Revelation 20:5–6)

2. Postmillennialists are seeking a Christianized world, a one thousand-year reign of righteous government before Christ's return—a view that influences today's American political process in no small part.

3. The premillennial view states that the one thousand-year period of Revelation is a literal millennium. Jesus Christ will revive Israel into the political, moral, and spiritual authority on Earth, the head of the nations she was supposed to have been, having fallen short of that status due to corporate and individual sin. The premillennial view is the simplest exposition of the many Scriptures describing the return of Christ by the Old Testament prophets.

- A host of blessings befall Israel according to the premillennial view: the third temple, cleansed of Antichrist's filth, is glorious and effectual for worship thanks to the Lord's presence as Messiah, King, and God ruling from the temple mount; Israel's ancestral lands are restored to descendants of the twelve tribes; life spans increase immensely, and the holy city is brought to Eden-like splendor.

- Contrary to popular premillenial doctrine, however, I believe many of the millenarian blessings are localized to the Jewish people and that unbelievers taking the mark during the tribulation enter under the rule of Christ with a rod of iron, compelling worship and obeisance. Who would Christ rule over if all those receiving the mark are thrown into Hell as the millennium starts leaving only true believers on Earth?

Chapter 17

"I Will Walk Among You and Be Your God"

Then the man and his wife heard the sound of the LORD God as he was walking in the garden in the cool of the day . . .
—Genesis 3:8a

Adam and Eve were created in a state of innocence, sinless, until they gave in to temptation and fell from grace into a state of sin. Adam was unique in all of creation, formed from the earth (Genesis 2:7), as a potter fashions a vessel from clay. The Lord breathed into His vessel's nostrils the breath of life, and man became a living creature (Genesis 2:7). The body of man is formed from the physical elements, but the breath of God formed man's spirit when he became a living mortal. Only man was created in the image of God (Genesis 1:27). Only man possesses a mind, exercises will, and feels a depth of emotions. Animals are instinctual and do not choose from conscience, live by moral code, or worship God. Only man was created for close personal relationship with God.

And they hid from the LORD God among the trees of the garden.
Genesis 3:8b

After he drove the man out, he placed on the east side of the Garden of Eden cherubim and a flaming sword flashing back and forth to guard the way to the tree of life. Genesis 3:24

When Adam and Eve sinned against God, their relationship with God was broken. God no longer walked with Adam and Eve—they were cast from His presence. As a result of sin entering the world, mankind and the earth were cursed. First Adam and Eve were separated from God by sin, immediately suffering spiritual death, and, eventually, their mortal bodies aged and died also. Paradise was lost. God's desire to walk among His people never changed, however, and the purpose of God's plan of redemption is the restoration of men so God may once more walk among His people.

How did God affect His covenant with a chosen people? One important step in the restoration of personal intimacy with man was God's establishment of a covenant relationship with the man Abram. Abram was seventy-five years old when he was called by God to leave his country, his people, and his household (Genesis 12:1–4). The Lord pledged to bless Abram and said:

"I will make you into a great nation and I will bless you; I will make your name great, and you will be a blessing. I will bless those who bless you, and whoever curses you I will curse; and all peoples on earth will be blessed through you." Genesis 12:2–3

Abram took his spouse, Sarai, a nephew, Lot, and their servants, flocks, and herds to Canaan. As years passed Abram was indeed blessed by God. During a famine in Canaan, Abram traveled to Egypt (Genesis 12:10). Despite some difficulties there, Abram returned to Canaan having acquired many livestock and servants (Genesis 12:16). After a time, Abram and his nephew Lot had so many possessions they felt they had to separate since the land could not support them both (Genesis 13:6). Although Abram was blessed with massive wealth and success over his enemies (Genesis 14:20), childless, he grieved over his lack of an heir. Sarai was well beyond childbearing years, yet the Lord promised Abram a natural heir—a son from Abram's own body:

> He took him outside and said, "Look up at the heavens and count the stars—if indeed you can count them." Then he said to him, "So shall you offspring be." Abram believed the LORD, and he credited to him as righteousness. Genesis 15:5–6

Abram was promised that all peoples on Earth would be blessed through him (Genesis 12:3). He promised a natural heir and numerous offspring (Genesis 15:4–5). By faith, Abram received God's gracious promise of the promised Messiah through his genealogical line (John 8:56). Abram is therefore a "father," or antecedent, of all who believe in Christ by faith (Romans 4:11–23).

God promised Abram's natural descendants would accede to perpetual possession of the land of Canaan (Genesis 15:18–21). He confirmed His promise by cutting a covenant with Abram (Genesis 15:10–18). The term, "cutting a covenant," stems from a common practice among ancient peoples. When two parties agreed to contractual obligation, their agreement was ratified while slaying an animal or animals. After the animal's death, its body would be divided into halves and each of the parties would walk between the butchered pieces and declare: "If I break my pledge, may it be so done (split in two parts) to me!"

> When Abram was ninety-nine years old, the LORD appeared to him and said, "I am God Almighty, walk before me and be blameless. I will confirm my covenant between me and you and will greatly increase your numbers." Abram fell face down, and God said to him, "As for me, this is my covenant with you: You will

be the father of many nations. No longer will you be called Abram; your name will be Abraham, for I have made you a father of many nations." Genesis 17:1–5

How is Abram related to all faithful people? Abram means "exalted father" and is a lovely picture referring to God, Father and Giver of all life. Abraham means "father of many." This second name identified Abraham as the one whom God blessed as a patriarch of natural descendants and the father of those saved through faith. Abraham's progeny include the twelve tribes of Israel and the Arab peoples (Genesis 25:13–16). Those who come to a saving faith in Christ are called the spiritual seed of Abraham (Romans 9:8; Galatians 3:29) and comprise the spiritual offspring of Abraham.

> "This is my covenant with you and your descendants after you, the covenant you are to keep: Every male among shall be circumcised. You are to undergo circumcision, and it will be the sign of the covenant between me and you." Genesis 17:10–11

The ceremony of circumcision is called a *b'riyt*, a Hebrew word that may be translated as "a cutting." Circumcision is performed on a Jewish male child when he is eight days old and is a physical sign in one's flesh as a reminder of the covenant God "cut" with Abraham. As a religious ritual, it was to be observed by Abraham's physical seed only.

Paul admonished gentile men attending alongside Jewish believers in churches in the Roman province of Galatia not to undergo circumcision (Galatians 5:2–6). Judaizers insisted that all ceremonial practices of the Mosaic Law were binding on all Christians and influenced these Gentiles. Gentiles do not become physical Jews or replace Israel through trusting in Christ, the Jewish Messiah. By faith, they become spiritual sons of Abraham, an example of a faithful person. A true sign of reconciliation to God is not a sign in the flesh but circumcision of the heart (Romans 2:28–29). Inward circumcision is regeneration of the heart by the power of the Holy Spirit.

> God also said to Abraham, "As for Sarai your wife, you are to no longer call her Sarai; her name will be Sarah. I will bless her and will surely give you a son by her." Genesis 17:15–16

Both Sarai and Sarah mean "princess." Sarai was renamed by God soon after Abram trusted in God by faith, to emphasize her motherhood of nations and kings of kingdoms.

> Now the LORD was gracious to Sarah as he had said, and the LORD did for Sarah what he had promised. Sarah became pregnant and bore a son to Abraham in His old age, at the very time God had promised him. Abraham gave the name Isaac to the son Sarah bore him. Genesis 21:1–3

Isaac means "laughter." Sarah laughed to herself in disbelief when she overheard God's promise to open her barren womb (Genesis 18:11–12). Isaac would be born to a ninety-year-old woman and her one hundred-year-old husband. Nothing is too difficult for God! The miraculous birth of Isaac, son of promise, foreshadowed the miraculous birth of Jesus, Son of David. God in His desire to restore an intimate and personal relationship with man first established a covenant relationship with Abraham. That covenant was extended and reconfirmed to Abraham's descendants, Isaac, and Isaac's son, Jacob.

> God said to him, "Your name is Jacob, but you will no longer be called Jacob; your name will be Israel." So he named him Israel. And God said to him, "I am God Almighty, be fruitful and in-

crease in number. A nation and a community of nations will come from you, and kings will come from your body. The land I gave to Abraham and Isaac I also give to you, and I will give this land to your descendants after you." Genesis 35:10–12

Just as the birth of Isaac would occur at the very time God had promised it would, so the nation of Israel would be delivered out of the bondage of Egypt—according to God's prophetic timetable.

> Then the LORD said to him [Abraham], "Know for certain that your descendants will be strangers in a country not their own, and they will be enslaved and mistreated four hundred years. But afterward they will come out with great possessions." Genesis 15:13–14

The covenant the Lord cut with Abram was unconditional, regarding any extended effort on Abram's part. Abram fell into a deep sleep while God, in the form of a smoking fire pot with a blazing torch, passed between the pieces of the slaughtered animals of their contract (Genesis 15:12–17). The Abrahamic Covenant is based on the perfect faithfulness of God alone and His ability to fulfill His promises.

In a similar way, when the twelve tribes of Israel were set free from Egyptian captivity, they were brought to Mount Sinai, as God had promised Moses in advance (Exodus 3:12). Once more, God would confirm a covenant with chosen men. The Mosaic Covenant would be a conditional agreement limited to the nation of Israel. Israel would be blessed or cursed in accordance to their obedience or disobedience to the commands and decrees of God (Deuteronomy 30:19).

> When Moses went and told the people all the LORD's words and laws, they responded with one voice, "Everything the LORD has

said we will do." . . . Moses then took the blood, sprinkled it on the people and said, "This is the blood of the covenant that the Lord has made with you in accordance with all these words." Exodus 24:8

The Mosaic Covenant is known as the Law. The word *law* has been translated from the Hebrew word *Torah*. Torah is more accurately translated "instruction." Torah, or law, is thus understood to mean "learning to walk on a righteous path" or "pointing in the right direction." The Five Books of Moses, called the Pentateuch, make up the Torah. Although blessings or curses on the nation depend upon Israel's faithfulness or rebellion to the *Mosaic* Covenant, Israel's land rights are *perpetual* and *unconditional* according to the *Abrahamic* Covenant.

[Author's note: It is inaccurate to refer to all the Old Testament books as "Torah." The books of the Old Testament were known at the time of Christ as "the law and the prophets," and to the Jewish people today as an acronym, *Tanakh. Tanakh* is derived from the initial letters of the names of the three divisions of the modern Hebrew Bible: the Torah (five books of Moses); Nevi'im (the prophets); Ketuvim (the writings—poetic and historic books).]

How is Israel's relationship with God demonstrative of God's faithful followers?

"Then have them make a sanctuary for me, and I will dwell among them. Make this tabernacle and all its furnishings exactly like the pattern I will show you." Exodus 25:8–9

"I will walk among you and be your God, and you will be my people." Leviticus 26:12

God's desire and purpose to renew a personal relationship with man was manifested by His divine presence dwelling among His chosen people, Israel. *Tabernacle* is literally translated "dwelling place." A permanent sanctuary replaced the tabernacle, a portable tent of meeting. Solomon, who built the sanctuary, said of his more permanent temple:

> "But will God really dwell on earth with man? The heavens, even the highest heavens, cannot contain you. How much less this temple I have built!" 1 Kings 8:27

God is greater than His creation. The highest heavens cannot contain all His glory! Yet God, who is omnipresent, manifested a visible presence in the most holy place in the temple. Due to Israel's rebellion, however, God was provoked to jealousy by idolatry inside the temple, and God's visible glory departed from the temple and from Jerusalem (Ezekiel 10:18).

> For whoever keeps the whole law and yet stumbles at just one point is guilty of breaking all of it. James 2:10

It is impossible for any individual, except Christ, to live a perfect life without breaking any of God's law at some juncture. The nation of Israel had to institute a system of sacrifice to make atonement for inevitable transgressions of God's law. One purpose of God's law was to demonstrate to man the impossibility of attaining righteousness by works of the law itself (Galatians 2:16; Ephesians 2:9). The law makes individuals conscious of sin (Romans 3:20). The law points to the need of salvation, foreshadowed better things to come, and was fulfilled in Christ (Romans 3:20; 10:4; Galatians 3:24; Colossians 2:17).

> "Therefore the LORD himself will give you a sign: The virgin will be with child and will give birth to a son, and will call him Immanuel." Isaiah 7:14

> The Word became flesh and made His dwelling among us. John 1:14a

Immanuel means "God with us." Jesus, the living Word, made His dwelling among us in living flesh—God "tabernacled with man." Jesus visited us to pay a price He did not owe; we owed a debt we could not pay—for sin. Christ instituted His new covenant in His own blood (Luke 22:20). The old, Mosaic covenant for the Israelites contained regulations for worship and an earthly sanctuary (Hebrews 9:1).

When Christ came as high priest, He entered the most holy place in God's heavenly tabernacle through His own blood (Hebrews 9:11–12). The Mosaic Law could never save an individual by offering forgiveness for sin. It is impossible for the blood of animals to remove sin (Hebrews 10:4). The blood of sacrificial animals served as a mere temporary covering of sin. Animal sacrifices were needed to be performed for each instance of sin! God has today set aside the former covenant, as it is weak, and the law perfected nothing and no one (Hebrews 7:18).

How is Christ's new covenant superior to the Old Testament code of law? The new covenant of Christ is superior to the old and founded on better promises (Hebrews 8:6). By the power of Christ's atoning blood, He provides for the removal of sin. Unlike old covenant promises, the new covenant fulfills unconditionally granted and eternal promises. Christians are not under the yoke of the law but are set at freedom by God's grace. The good news regarding this covenant is the power of God for salvation of anyone who places trust in Christ (see Romans 1:16). God's plan for wayward man's reconciliation to Him is accomplished through Christ's finished work on the cross (John 19:30). On the cross, Christ poured out blood, confirming this magnificent new covenant (Luke 22:20).

Due to sin, Adam and Eve died spiritually, separated from God. Adam, as the federal head of man, brought death to all men through sin (1 Corinthians 15:22). One result of Adam's disobedience was a curse placed on man and the earth. Adam and Eve were cast from Eden and were denied access to God's tree of life. Christians, as partakers of the new covenant, however, will eat of the leaves of the heavenly tree of life and fully enjoy its fruit (Revelation 22:2). No longer will there be *any* curse (see Revelation 22:3). For Christians, intimate relationship with God is restored for eternity. God will again walk among His people. On the other hand, those who reject Christ remain separate from God eternally and suffer unending punishment and regret, something horrible to contemplate.

Summary of Chapter Seventeen

- Christ's Second Coming is the hope of restoration to incredible fellowship with God for all Christians.
- Fellowship was severed in the fall of Eden. One of God's primary steps to reconcile man to Him was through the selection of Abram who, by faith, provided a genealogy for Christ, the Messiah of all who believe by faith.
- The Abrahamic covenant of circumcision reminds us that God cuts covenants with the slaying of sacrifices and the outpouring of blood—Christ has given us His blood as God's penultimate redemptive act.
- God's Mosaic Law system, embodied in the Torah (five books of Moses), points to the individual's sullied conscience due to sin—redemption from guilt under the law is found in God's new covenant.
- God walked in fellowship alongside Adam and Eve in Eden. God walked through the slain pieces of animal sacrifice when confirming His covenant with Abram. The second Adam, Jesus Christ, will walk among His people in the coming eternal kingdom, forever.

Chapter 18

The Lord Chooses Jerusalem (Again!)

"Shout and be glad, O Daughter of Zion. For I am coming, and I will live among you," declares the LORD. "Many nations will be joined with the LORD in that day and will become my people. I will live among you and you will know that the LORD Almighty has sent me to you. The LORD will inherit Judah as His portion in the holy land and will again choose Jerusalem."

—Zechariah 2:10–12

And they sang a new song: "You are worthy to take the scroll and to open its seals, because you were slain, and with your blood you purchased men for God from every tribe and language and people and nation. You have made them to be a kingdom and priests to serve our God, and they will reign on earth."

—Revelation 5:9–10

When Jesus returns to establish His earthly kingdom, He will again choose Jerusalem as God's special dwelling place. As Jesus returns from Heaven to redeem the surviving remnant of Israel, He will be joined with God's blood-bought and glorified saints from every people on Earth. The people joined to the Lord will rule and reign with Christ during the millennium. Following the rapture, Christians will be judged in Heaven for degree of reward, celebrate at the wedding supper of the Lamb, and complete God's bridal week in Heaven, before returning to Earth (see Genesis 29:27; 2 Corinthians 5:10; Revelation 19:7).

One objection raised regarding the post-tribulation rapture view (the belief that Christ raptures Christians *after* the seven-year tribulation period) is that it allows little time for rewarding the saints or for the Lamb's wedding supper. However, my contention is that the Church is raptured on the Feast of Trumpets, and Christ returns some days later with His saints, on the Day of Atonement. This would account for a time span of ten days, allowing perhaps for three days of judgment and reward and a literal seven-day bridal celebration! This particular "pre-wrath" view of the rapture is based on my understanding that the "days of great distress" are cut short, ended prematurely, for the elect's sake (true believers). The rapture thus occurs before the end, not at the very end, of the seven-year tribulation period.

How does the Israelite wedding tradition picture the coming return of Jesus Christ to Earth? Knowledge of Hebrew wedding traditions, such as the bridal week, is helpful in clarifying and interpreting biblical concepts. Familiarity with the culture and customs of Bible times helps strengthen an understanding of passages touching on Christ's relationship to His Church. We can also gain deeper understanding of the parables relating to Christ's return and the establishing of His earthly kingdom.

In typical ancient Israelite ceremonies, prearranged marriages were set by the bridal couple's family. A friend of the bridegroom negotiated on behalf of the groom and his father with the designated representative of the bride's father. An appropriate dowry was determined, and the bride's father was invited to use the interest from a dowry but could not spend the principal sum. The dowry was held in trust for the bride in case of her becoming widowed or divorced. In compensation for the loss of the daughter's work, a contribution to helping her household, a "bride's price" was paid to the bride's family by the groom.

The traditional Jewish wedding ceremony consisted of two segments. The first part, *kiddushin*, is a betrothal. During the betrothal ceremony, two benedictions are shared, the first one over a cup of wine. Following the blessing and sharing of the wine, the bridegroom gives the bride an object of value in the presence of at least two witnesses. The bridegroom recites the marriage formula: "Behold, you are consecrated unto me according to the Law of Moses and Israel." After the groom said these words, a second benediction is recited. This second blessing is offered to help enable the couple to remain chaste during their engagement.

The second portion of the wedding ceremony is the *nissu'in*, or marriage proper. In the case of a young maiden who has never married, the nissu'in took place one year after the kiddushin betrothal. A formal marriage contract written in Aramaic (the language of the Babylonian captivity, later used in Israel) was signed. This ketubba contract literally means, "that which is written." Since religious law permitted Jewish men to divorce at any time and for any reason, the ketubba was introduced to protect the woman's rights, by changing an easily attainable divorce into a financially costly matter for the divorcing husband. The conditions stipulated in the ketubba also guaranteed the woman's right to property when her husband died. A ketubba written for a widow or divorcee being married would be less valuable than that for a virgin.

During the betrothal year, the bridegroom would return to his father's home to build the couple's new home nearby, while the bride prepared her wedding clothes. In the case of a wealthy family, clothes would be provided for all of the wedding guests! Since the couple would be anxious to consummate their marriage, the father of the groom would have to approve the construction of their honeymoon cottage and would be the final authority as to when the bridegroom could return to his fiancée's home for his bride.

According to the Babylonian Talmud (volumes of rabbinical commentaries on the Mosaic Law and Jewish tradition), participation in the marriage ceremony and attendant celebrations was considered a good thing and a good deed. Those entertaining the bride and groom are compared to a believer who had sacrificed a thanksgiving offering to God (see Babylonian Talmud, Bereshit 6b). The bridegroom was required to devote at least three days' preparation to his wedding feast. Even if a parent of the wedding couple died on the set day of the marriage, its consummation took place and the funeral was held afterward (Babylonian Talmud, Ketubba 3a).

The bride and the bridegroom were dressed like royalty for their nuptials. The groom would wear a crown and the bride would often work a circlet of coins from her dowry into her headdress. The rites of marriage were held under a *huppa*, a wedding canopy. The huppa symbolizes the bride cohabiting with the groom at their home. Benedictions were recited, and later that evening, a processional would move from the bride's house, where the wedding ceremony took place, to the new home prepared by the groom.

The bride's veil would be removed and then placed upon the shoulders of the groom. A declaration was made of the groom that "the government will be upon his shoulders." The young maidens in attendance would carry long poles with lighted, oil-soaked rags on top. After consummation of the marriage, there was an exhibition of evidence of the bride's virginity; a bloodstained sheet or garment of clothing was presented to the assemblage (see Deuteronomy 22:13–17). A bridal week ensued, which included seven days of joyous feasting and merriment (Genesis 29:27).

Jewish traditions and customs associated with marriage indeed echo the Scriptures referring to Christ and the Church:

> To this John replied, "A man can receive only what is given him
> from heaven. You yourselves can testify that I said, 'I am not the
> Christ but am sent ahead of him.' The bride belongs to the bride-
> groom. The friend who attends the bridegroom waits and listens
> for him, and is full of joy when he hears the bridegroom's voice.
> That joy is mine, and it is now complete. He must become greater,
> I must become less." John 3:27–30

John's disciples came to John voicing their concern that Jesus
was baptizing, although in fact it was not Jesus who baptized, but
His disciples (John 4:2). John responded to their concern by drawing an analogy between his baptismal ministry and the role of the
"best man" at a wedding. John demonstrated that the most important man at a wedding is not the friend attending the groom but is
certainly the bridegroom, of course. The disciples of John were
not to be dismayed or jealous of Jesus' growing following. "The
bride belongs to the bridegroom" indicates that the Church of true
believers is the bride of Christ. John, in his role as friend of the
groom, represented God the Father, allegorically. God, like the
friend of the groom, determines the bride's dowry price.

In the same vein, John's water baptism was one of repentance,
a ministry helping prepare hearts to receive the Savior. John referred to Jesus as the "Lamb of God who takes away the sin of the
world" (John 1:29). The price the groom paid to purchase His
bride, the Church? the pouring out of His own blood (Revelation
5:9).

Note carefully the comparisons. The *first coming of Christ* fulfilled the betrothal, or *first part of the marriage ceremony*. The betrothal included the reciting of a benediction and the sharing of a
cup of wine:

> Then he [Jesus Christ] took the cup, gave thanks and offered it
> to them, saying, "Drink from it, all of you." Matthew 26:27

During the ceremony, the groom gave the bride a bride gift in the presence of two witnesses:

> On one occasion, while he was eating with them, he gave them this command: "Do not leave Jerusalem, but wait for the gift my Father promised, which you have heard me speak about. For John baptized with water, but in a few days you will be baptized with the Holy Spirit." Acts 1:4–5

> "I tell you the truth: It is for your good that I am going away. Unless I go away, the counselor will not come to you; but if I go, I will send him to you." John 16:7

When Jesus ascended to Heaven, He sat down at the right hand of God the Father (Hebrews 1:3). The bride's gift, the promised Holy Spirit, was given to the Church on Pentecost in the presence of two heavenly witnesses—God the Father and Jesus Christ.

The *second part of the wedding ceremony* will take place *after Christ returns to gather His elect in the air at the rapture.* In biblical times, the bridegroom spent one year building a home so he and his bride could live together comfortably.

During the church age, what is Christ doing for His bride?

> "Do not let your hearts be troubled. Trust in God; trust also in me. In my Father's house are many rooms; if it were not so, I would have told you. I am going there to prepare a place for you. And if I go and prepare a place for you, I will come back and take you to be with me that you also may be where I am." John 14:1–3

The bridegroom awaits the Father's approval on the bride's dwelling place so He may return for His bride.

"No one knows about that day or hour, not even the angels in heaven, nor the Son, but only the Father." Matthew 24:36

Just as a betrothed young maiden knew it would take one year for the bridegroom to return, but did not know exactly when he would be ready, the Church will not know the exact day or hour but will know the approximate return of the Lord.

During the time interval between betrothal and the wedding proper, the bride made her wedding clothes.

"Let us rejoice and be glad and give him glory! For the wedding of the Lamb has come, and His bride has made herself ready. Fine linen, bright and clean, was given her to wear. (Fine linen stands for the righteous acts of the saints.)" Revelation 19:7–8

Compare Revelation's statement of the wedding to Isaiah's declaration:

I delight greatly in the Lord; my soul rejoices in my God. For he has clothed me with garments of salvation and arrayed me in a robe of righteousness, as a bridegroom adorns His head like a priest, and as a bride adorns herself with her jewels. Isaiah 61:10

The bride has made herself ready in Revelation 19 by removing filthy, sin-stained garments and being robed in righteousness of Christ, by faith. The bridegroom wears a crown of beauty or priestly turban. Christ, King of Kings, our high priest and last and greatest of the prophets, has a worthily-fashioned bride. Jesus, who fulfills these three anointed offices in one person, will be dressed as king, priest, and prophet at the wedding supper of the Lamb.

Often, as mentioned, the Israelite bride would decorate her headdress with coins from her dowry.

"Suppose a woman has ten silver coins and loses one. Does she not light a lamp, sweep the house and search carefully until she finds it? And when she finds it, she calls her friends and neighbors together and says, 'Rejoice with me; I have found my lost coin.'" Luke 15:8–9

To the casual reader, it may seem that the woman's reaction in the parable to the loss of a single coin was extreme. If the lost coin was part of her dowry and for her wedding headdress, however, her rejoicing at finding the coin is quite understandable. She gathered her friends and neighbors to share her joy—like a wedding celebration. In a similar way, God rejoices in the presence of the holy angels whenever even one person trusts in Him by faith and is "found."

According to Jewish wedding tradition, the bridegroom was required to devote at least three days to the preparation of the wedding feast. The feast itself lasted seven days. If my understanding is correct, Christ will rapture the Church on the Feast of Trumpets. Ten days later, on the Day of Atonement, He will return to Earth with His saints. These ten days could allow for a literal three days of preparation (judgment of the Church for reward) and a subsequent, literal seven-day wedding feast.

How does the Feast of Tabernacles picture the gathering of saints at the rapture? Three times each year, all Jewish men were required to return to Jerusalem to attend worship at the temple. In Jesus' day, Jerusalem overflowed with Jewish people from across the Roman Empire during Passover, Pentecost, and the Feast of Tabernacles. Passover is a picture of the bridal price. The bride of Christ (the Church) was purchased (redeemed) by His own blood. Pentecost portrays giving a bridal gift—the Holy Spirit poured upon and into the Church. And Tabernacles? The Feast of Tabernacles is a picture of both the wedding and subsequent dwelling together of the heavenly bride and groom—the Lamb's supper and millennial reign of Christ and His saints.

> "So beginning with the fifteenth day of the seventh month, after you have gathered the crops of the land, celebrate the festival to the LORD for seven days; the first day is a day of rest, and the eighth day is also a day of rest . . . Live in booths for seven days: All native-born Israelites are to live in booths so your descendants will know that I had the Israelites live in booths when I brought them out of Egypt. I am the LORD your God." Leviticus 23:29, 42–43

The tabernacle booth, a *succa*, is constructed with latticework and decorated with fruit and leaves from the seasonal harvest. It looks quite similar to the Jewish wedding huppa. The Feast of Tabernacles, called *Sukkot*, is celebrated with seven days' feasting and dancing—in much the same way as the bridal week/honeymoon/feast is celebrated. The Feast of Tabernacles celebration follows the wheat and grape harvests. I understand that the wedding supper of the Lamb is celebrated after the rapture, which divides man into two camps (symbolized by the wheat harvest separating wheat from chaff) and the treading of the grapes in the wine press of God's wrath (see Revelation 14:19–20).

> Then the survivors from all nations that have attacked Jerusalem will go up year after year to worship the King, the LORD Almighty, and to celebrate the Feast of Tabernacles. Zechariah 14:16

What of Christ's return to Earth following the rapture and subsequent reward of the saints? After the wedding supper of the Lamb, Christ returns with His bride to Earth to subdue the nations. He will establish His Messianic kingdom on Earth. During the millennium, survivors will worship Christ and celebrate the Feast of

Tabernacles each year. I believe this is not a willing act of devotion of the survivors from the nations. They have taken the mark of the beast and are enemies of Christ, coerced to come and worship by threat of dire punishment.

> If any of the peoples of the earth do not go up to Jerusalem to worship the King, the LORD Almighty, they will have no rain. Zechariah 14:17

The Lord will choose Jerusalem anew as His dwelling place and the center of His theocracy. He will rule the nations with a rod of iron from Zion. God will tabernacle with men and men will celebrate the Feast of Tabernacles annually and offer oblation to God.

Jerusalem is a holy city for three monotheistic faiths—Judaism, Christianity, and Islam. Jerusalem has come to mean "city of peace," as "salem" is associated with the Hebrew word, *shalom*, which means "peace." From the time of Joshua to the destruction of Jerusalem by Titus in A.D. 70, Jerusalem has been frequented with revolt, siege, famine, and brutalities of war. After the Roman army destroyed the city, slaughtering many of its Jewish inhabitants, the Romans began to refortify Jerusalem. Again, Jerusalem would be the center of revolution. Jewish people under the leadership of Bar Kochba, a false messiah, failed to overthrow their Roman oppressors from A.D. 132–A.D. 135.

Nearly two centuries later, the so-called conversion of Constantine the Great (many scholars believe Constantine never sincerely placed His trust in Christ) ushered in a period of peace and prosperity for Jerusalem and many famous shrines were erected there. In A.D. 614, the Persians invaded Jerusalem again, and the inhabitants of the city were massacred. In A.D. 969, control of the city passed to the Shiite caliphs of Egypt. In 1010, the caliph ordered the destruction of numerous Christian shrines. In 1071, the

Turks defeated the Byzantines and displaced the Egyptians as masters of the Holy Land, cutting the pilgrim routes through the Holy Land. This action prompted the Crusades. For a period of nearly two centuries, from 1096 until 1270, the Crusades were undertaken by Europeans to recapture Jerusalem from the hands of the Moslems, besides other less laudable objectives. In 1517, the Ottoman sultan, Selim I, took the city, inaugurating a Turkish regime that lasted 400 years, until World War I.

In 1917, British troops entered Jerusalem after the retreat of the Turks. This era lasted until 1948 when Israel declared nationhood, an act affirmed by the United Nations. Jerusalem was then divided between Transjordan and the Israelis. During the Six-Day War of June 1967, the Israelis stormed the Old City quarter of Jerusalem and claimed a unified city, under Jewish authority once again after more than 2,500 years. Today the "city of peace" is assaulted by terrorists and is a center of world attention. The PLO desires to divide the city and then claim Jerusalem as its own capital.

Although Jerusalem has been the geographic center of thousands of years of warfare, the bloodiest city on Earth, the Bible promises its restoration as a city of peace and the center of a peaceful, thousand-year empire.

> He (Messiah) will judge between the nations and will settle disputes for many peoples. They will beat their swords into plowshares and their spears into pruning hooks. Nation will not take up sword against nation, nor will they train for war anymore.
> Isaiah 2:4

This time of world peace occurs during the millennium, and, as many have failed to notice, following Armageddon. The dramatic events following the millennium will be discussed in the next chapter.

Summary of Chapter Eighteen

- When Jesus returns to establish His earthly kingdom, He will again choose Jerusalem as God's special dwelling place.

- Knowledge of Hebrew wedding traditions, such as the bridal week, is helpful in clarifying and interpreting biblical concepts regarding Christ's return. Note below the many comparisons between the traditional Jewish engagement and wedding with Christ's coming return.

  o Before the engagement:

  - Marriage pre-arranged by parents
  - God founds the Church through Christ (John 3:16)
  - Groom's friend negotiates on groom's behalf for a dowry for the bride
  - John the Baptist acts as bridegroom's friend and attendant, a "best man" (John 3:29)

  o Dowry held in trust:

  - The bride's father invited to use the interest from a dowry but could not spend the principal sum
  - Christians receive an imperishable inheritance from which they derive numerous blessings (Ephesians 1:11–12)
  - Dowry held in trust for bride in case of her becoming widowed or divorced

- The Holy Spirit is a deposit of the Christian's inheritance (Ephesians 1:13–14)
- Dowry paid as compensation for the loss of daughter's contribution to helping her household
- Christians rest from good works for their blood-bought salvation from Christ (Hebrews 4:10)

o Engagement ceremony:

- The betrothal ceremony includes prayer, benedictions, and a cup of wine
- Christ instituted communion in His new covenant (Matthew 26:27)
- Following the blessing and sharing of the wine, the bridegroom gives the bride an object of value in the presence of at least two witnesses
- Christ promised to grant the Holy Spirit to His assembled disciples during the Passover over a cup of wine (John 14:17)
- A special blessing is offered to help enable the betrothed couple to remain chaste during their engagement
- Christ is preparing for Himself a pure bride (Revelation 21:19–27)
- A ketubba protected the woman's rights by changing an easily attainable divorce into a financially costly matter for the divorcing husband

- Christ compared the Church to a treasure of great price: His death and resurrection (Matthew 13:46)
- The conditions stipulated in the ketubba guaranteed the woman's right to property when her husband died
- Christians receive blessings from the covenant/testament of Christ's atoning death (1 Thessalonians 5:10)
- A ketubba written for a widow or divorcee would be less valuable than one for a virgin
- Christians are admonished to remain spiritually and morally pure (1 Corinthians 6:15)

o Preparation made during the engagement period:

- During the betrothal year, the bridegroom would return to his father's home to build the couple's new home nearby while the bride prepared her wedding clothes
- Christ prepares our heavenly home near Father God's dwelling place (John 14:2) while His church performs good works in His absence, which adorns it with blessing (Revelation 19:14)
- The groom's father, the final authority as to when the bridegroom could return to his fiancée's home for his bride, approves the construction of their honeymoon cottage
- Christ builds our home while awaiting the Father's commission to return (Matthew 24:36)

o   The wedding ceremony:

- The bride and the bridegroom were dressed like royalty for their nuptials—the groom would wear a crown and the bride would often work a circlet of coins from her dowry into her headdress
- The wedding party in Heaven is gloriously attired (Revelation 19:8)
- In the case of a wealthy family, clothes would be provided for all of the wedding guests
- Christ has many glorified attendants at the heavenly wedding to His Church (Matthew 22:8–12)
- The rites of marriage were held under a wedding canopy, symbolizing the bride cohabiting with the groom at their home—a processional would move from the bride's house, where the wedding ceremony took place, to the new home prepared by the groom
- Christians await a rapture away from the earth into the air, and then, to Heaven (1 Corinthians 15:51–53)
- Young maidens in attendance at the wedding would carry long poles with lighted, oil-soaked rags on top in a processional
- Christians are compared to lights enlightening others' path to salvation and true knowledge (Matthew 10:27)
- The bride's veil would be removed and placed on the groom's shoulders—a declaration was made of the groom that "The government will be upon his shoulders"

- Christ bears just government and lifts the veil of ignorance regarding His nature for His bride (Isaiah 9:6; 2 Corinthians 3:14–16)
- The bridegroom recites the marriage formula, "Behold, you are consecrated unto me according to the Law of Moses and Israel"
- Christ fulfills the law and so redeems believers from the curse for disobeying it (Matthew 5:17)

o The wedding is consummated by the couple and celebrated by the community:

- The couple would be anxious to consummate their marriage
- The blessed hope is Christ's return for His bride (1 Peter 1:3)
- After consummation of the marriage, there was an exhibition of evidence of the bride's virginity
- Christ demonstrates the purity of the Church to the world upon His return (1 Peter 2:12)
- The bridegroom was required to devote at least three days' preparation to his wedding feast, and a typical celebration, following the nuptials lasted seven days for everyone
- We are looking at a prophetic timetable of ten Days of Awe between the rapture and return of Christ, for preparation and a great feast

- The Feast of Tabernacles ushers in separation of wheat from chaff and the pressing of grapes
- A tremendous allusion to the coming separation of people and outpoured wrath of God, which I believe will happen at a soon-coming Feast of Tabernacles!

Chapter 19

Millennium's End

When the thousand years are over, Satan will be released from His prison and will go out to deceive the nations in the four corners of the earth—Gog and Magog—to gather them for battle. In number they are like the sand of the seashore.

—Revelation 20:7–8

At the beginning of the millennial reign of Christ on Earth, Satan will be bound and cast into the Abyss, which will then be locked and sealed. The seal across the lock to the Abyss signifies the approval, omnipotent power, and ultimate authority of Almighty God restricting Satan to the bottomless pit for imprisonment. During the millennium, Satan will be greatly restricted from deceiving, tempting, or accusing man.

What is the devil up to today? We are presently living in an evil time (Ephesians 5:16) when the devil is working his schemes in persons disobedient to Christ (Ephesians 2:2). Since sin entered the world through Adam, there have always been evil acts committed by men. As time draws near to the return of the Lord, the days become increasingly more evil (Matthew 24:12). In ages past, classical works of art, theater, and orchestral music were typically based on biblical themes or inspired by creation's beauty. Western culture, a reflection of those influences, was refined and dignified. There was a strong work ethic for everyone. Etiquette, chivalry, and courtesy were stressed and those in authority were respected. Families were held intact and moral values were cherished and abided by for most people.

Today the media ranks as the primary influence upon our culture. Daily, we are assailed by a relentless barrage of visual and auditory messages touting greed, sex, and violence. What are the inevitable results of our media madness? Our senses are stimulated and imaginations provoked to lust after worldly things and to fulfill the desires of the flesh. Technological advances in the electronics and computing industries have made access to gross pornography, acts of pedophilia and degradation of men and women, and depiction of graphic sadistic violence, available to even the youngest of children. Satan is the ruler of the kingdom of the air (Ephesians 2:2), a title indicating, as does his authority over a fallen world, his ability to pervert our culture through the popular media. He has been successful in using the airwaves to reach our homes to expose us to smut and perversity in the guise of entertainment.

> The woman said, "The serpent deceived me, and I ate." Genesis 3:13b

During the millennium, Christ will reign in righteousness and administer justice. Those who are living during this period of unprecedented peace and tranquility, unlike Eve, will be unable to claim that they were tempted or deceived by Satan!

What happens to the world when Satan's millennial imprisonment ends? When Satan is released at the end of His one thousand-year term of confinement, he will have little difficulty in raising a vast army and gathering representatives from the nations for battle. Symbolically, Satan and his end-time horde are described as "Gog" and "Magog." Gog is the chief prince of Meshech and Tubal (Ezekiel 38:2), lands to the north of Israel. The attack against Israel during the tribulation by a northern army (probably Russia) and her allies (Ezekiel 38:5–6) "Persia" (Iran), "Cush" (Ethiopia), "Put" (Libya), "Gomer" (Germany), and "Beth Togarmah" (Turkey), typifies a last great rebellion of the nations that takes place at the millennium's end.

The survivors from the nations attacking Jerusalem (Zechariah 14:16) before the one thousand years have begun, enter the millennium brandishing the mark of the beast on their right hand or forehead (Revelation 13:16). Physically alive but spiritually dead, they have hearts of stone and are rebellious by nature. I believe that, for the most part, the children that they bear and raise will reflect the values of their ungodly parents. Christ rules in the midst of His enemies for one thousand years. When Satan is released, he deceives the nations into believing that they can launch a successful attack against Jerusalem!

> They marched across the breadth of the earth and surrounded the camp of God's people, the city he loves. But fire came down from heaven and devoured them. Revelation 20:9

During the time of Moses, God afflicted the land and people of Egypt with ten plagues. After the tenth plague passed and the first-born of Egypt had been struck by God, Pharaoh summoned Moses and Aaron. Pharaoh told Moses and Aaron in clear terms to take all the Hebrews and leave the land of Egypt (Exodus 12:29–32). At the time of the Exodus, there were nearly 600,000 Hebrew men, their wives, and children, who journeyed out of the land of bondage. Numerous Egyptians and others traveled with them in triumph and flight (Exodus 12:38).

The ten plagues progressively intensified over a period, and during the course of this dreadful time, reverence of God certainly impressed the Egyptians and their non-Hebrew slaves. The day before Egypt was to experience the worst hailstorm in history, Moses confronted Pharaoh for not allowing the Hebrews to leave and worship the Lord, and so:

> Those officials of Pharaoh who feared the word of the LORD hurried to bring their slaves and their livestock inside. But those who ignored the word of the LORD left their slaves and livestock in the field. Exodus 9:20–21

God is both merciful (Jeremiah 3:12, for one of many examples) and just (see 2 Thessalonians 1:6) in nature. A holy God, He requires a punishment for sin; yet in mercy, He withholds judgment for those willing to receive His grace. Not only were Hebrews delivered from oppression in Egypt but also many others took part in the Exodus. Gentiles who feared the Lord joined the Hebrew slaves to take refuge from the plague upon the firstborn in houses where lamb's blood was applied at the doorway (Exodus 12:7). Likewise, during the time of tribulation, people may refuse the mark of the beast and flee to spiritual refuge in Christ. Jews and Gentiles may pass from spiritual death to receive eternal life by applying the blood of the Lamb to the "door of their heart." The Egyptians witnessed that the plagues did not come upon the Hebrews who worked among them as slaves, and this testimony of the power and preservation of God convicted many to seek God. I am hopeful that the Church's endurance during the tribulation both purifies the Church and serves to convict many to refuse the mark of the beast and place their trust in Christ instead.

The parting of the sea with Moses, and subsequent crossing on dry land by a great mixed multitude, is an excellent picture of the coming rapture. All of God's people were gathered in one place, supernaturally delivered from the hands of Pharaoh (as a type of Antichrist) who avowed to destroy their lives. Led by Moses, a type of Christ, God poured final judgment upon the enemies of God's people. The water of judgment, which flowed over the Egyptians and their chariots and horses, is a picture of Revelation's bowls—God's wrath poured upon the earth.

The pattern of miraculous deliverance of God's people followed by immediate judgment of God's enemies is found elsewhere in the Bible. The day God shut Noah and his family inside the ark, for example, the deadly floodgates of water were opened on the earth (Genesis 7:10–16). The day Lot and his family were pulled from Sodom by angels, God rained burning sulfur on the wicked cities of the plain (Genesis 19:16–24). I believe that on the same day as the great and terrible day of the LORD begins (the Ten Days of Awe begin), the Church will be raptured and the final plagues poured on the earth.

> So they put slave masters over them to oppress them with forced labor and they built Pithom and Ramses as store cities for Pharaoh. But the more they were oppressed, the more they multiplied and spread; so the Egyptians came to dread the Israelites and worked them ruthlessly. Exodus 1:11–13

The furnace of affliction not only purifies disciples but tends to multiply their numbers. The tribulation not only purifies God's Church but will be a time of great growth in numbers for the Church—that is a great hope. Regarding the persecution of the Church, it is said "the blood of Christian martyrs is seed for many new believers."

It seems the plagues of Egypt, like the Revelation "trumpet judgments" of God, are hurled on the earth during the course of several days, even months. The great final rebellion of man, however, which takes place at the close of the millennium, will be judged quickly, with finality. Multitudes surrounding Jerusalem are devoured by fire from heaven. There is no time for repentance or further opportunity for forgiveness!

The physical death of the vast horde of warriors from the nations is followed by more grievous judgment still—a degree of eternal punishment for unbelievers from all times. Satan at one time initiated a rebellion in Heaven and a third of the angels fell with him (Revelation 12:4). At the end of the coming millennium, Satan leads a rebellion of the nations. Satan will reap what he has sown. The devil, tormentor of countless lives for ages, will be tormented for eternity.

> The devil, who deceived them, was thrown into the lake of burning sulfur, where the beast and the false prophet had been thrown. They will be tormented day and night for ever . . . Revelation 20:10

At the beginning of the millennium, the Antichrist and the False Prophet are thrown in the lake of burning sulfur. One thousand years later, Satan joins them both to be tormented eternally. Do you see it? The beast and false prophet have not died or been ultimately consumed in the lake of fire but still exist after one thousand years to enter an eternity of torment.

Scholars who deny the eternal nature of God's judgment have questioned a loving God who would dare to create an eternal Hell. Perhaps Hell is not a real place but symbolizes anguish, grief caused by the loss of goodness itself? The concept of a literal Hell does not make sense to scoffers nor does it occur to many that Jesus Christ would step out of heavenly glory, lower Himself to wear human flesh, and die an excruciating death (Philippians 2:5–8) to redeem sinful men.

Contrary to the popular view, Satan does not rule in Hell, nor does he personally inflict painful punishment on disobedient mankind. The original purpose of eternal fire was to punish the devil and his minions, and it is unfortunate that men are lost.

"Then he will say to those on His left, 'Depart from me, you who are cursed, into eternal fire prepared for the devil and His angels.'" Matthew 25:41

Those who by persistence in doing good seek glory, honor and immortality, he will give eternal life. But for those who are self-seeking and who reject the truth and follow evil, there will be wrath and anger. Romans 2:7–8

Those who trust Christ in this life follow their Lord into eternal glory. Those who reject Him who is truth (John 14:6) follow Satan into eternal torment.

Hell, the lake of fire, is a place of eternal torment where a sinner's "worm does not die" and Hell's fire is never quenched (Mark 9:48). Hell is called *Gehenna* in Greek, and derives this name from the valley of Hinnom, which is located south of Jerusalem.

In the valley of Hinnom, Solomon built an altar to the evil god Molech (see 1 Kings 11:5; 2 Kings 23:10). Molech was the Ammonites' chief deity, and Molech worship included the abhorrent practice of human sacrifice. In an attempt to curry Molech's favor, his worshipper would cast his or her living child into a burning furnace.

Molech worship was specifically forbidden in the law (Leviticus 18:21; 20:1–5), yet the evil Judean kings Ahaz and Manasseh sacrificed their own sons in fire to Molech (2 Kings 16:3; 21:6). In later times, Hinnom, or Gehenna, became Jerusalem's perpetual garbage dump where unclean refuge was found continually burning. Gehenna's refuse included unclean bodies not deserving a traditional burial. Every hour of the day and night Gehenna's smoke ascended, and vermin and worms writhed amongst the decaying flesh and bones of the lost.

If Hinnom and Gehenna picture fiery judgment, are there pictures of a physical location for Heaven in the Old Testament? *Sheol* is the Hebrew word for the grave, the realm of the dead. (*Hades* is the Greek equivalent of Sheol.) Before Christ's First Advent, Sheol, located inside the Earth, contained the souls of the departed. The righteous, in a place called Abraham's bosom (Luke 16:22) or paradise, enjoyed sweet fellowship with one another and rest for their souls. Unbelievers were tormented, separated from the righteous by an impassable gulf (Luke 16:23–26) to await final judgment.

> This is why it says: "When he ascended on high, he led captives in His train and gave gifts to men." What does 'he ascended' mean except that he also descended to the lower, earthly regions? Ephesians 4:8–9

> Jesus answered him, "I tell you the truth, today you will be with me in paradise." Luke 23:43

The apostle Paul spoke of a man caught up to the "third heaven" where the paradise of God is located (2 Corinthians 12:2–4). God created the *heavens* in the beginning (Genesis 1:1). We know from Scripture that the first heavens are our inner atmosphere where weather activity takes place (see Psalm 78:23). The highest Heaven, the third heaven of Paul's vision, is where God Himself dwells (1 Kings 8:27). We may logically conclude that the second heaven is the vast void of outer space and the cosmos surrounding the earth's atmosphere.

So, is Paradise under the earth now? Paradise, originally located inside Sheol, has been lifted to Heaven. At the cross, Jesus cried to the Father, as the Father had forsaken Him for our salvation (Matthew 27:46). Jesus, without sin, was made to be sin for us (2 Corinthians 5:21) and was separated from God. Jesus said His redemptive work was completed (John 19:30), and He commended His spirit into His Father's hands (Luke 23:46). I believe, as do most conservative scholars, that following His crucifixion, Jesus descended to the lower regions of Earth where paradise was located. When He ascended on high to Heaven, He "led captives in His train." Jesus thus brought righteous people, including a thief who expired on a cross beside Christ's, up to the third heaven. The wicked were left in Sheol, a spot more than the mere realm of the evil dead—a place of torment.

> Then I saw a great white throne and him who was seated on it. Earth and sky fled from His presence, and there was no place for them. And I saw the dead, great and small standing before the throne, and books were opened. Another book was opened, which is the book of life. The dead were judged according to what they had done as recorded in the books . . . death and Hades were thrown into the lake of fire. The lake of fire is the second death. If anyone's name was not found written in the book of life, he was thrown into the lake of fire. Revelation 20:11–12, 14–15

At the rapture, believers are blessed to take part in the *first* resurrection (Revelation 20:5). Following the one thousand year time period of the millennium, the rest of deceased humanity will be raised to life. For most, this will be a resurrection of those whose names are not seen in Heaven's book of life. These will be judged for degree of punishment according to their works. The wicked remain spiritually dead in sin and separated from God after their physical death. At the white throne judgment, these unfortunates are resurrected to life to stand in the presence of God. They are to be rejected, cast from God eternally to suffer separation from God for a second, final time.

A person is born again and has eternal life or else a person rejects Christ and remains spiritually dead. Heaven or Hell, eternal life or eternal death, is the choice. I pray, if you have not already done so, you will choose life (Deuteronomy 30:19) and trust in Jesus Christ's atoning death and resurrection for salvation.

Summary of Chapter Nineteen

- Satan rules the present world system and tempts men to sin. When the devil is bound for one thousand years, his temporal power will be severely limited—yet he will be released to attack God's people a final time.

- Clear patterns of miraculous deliverance of God's people, followed by immediate, subsequent judgment of God's enemies, are found in the Bible—Noah's deliverance before the flood, Lot's deliverance on the heels of Sodom's destruction, Pharaoh's armies drowned moments after the Hebrews and fleeing Gentiles went through the parted sea, etc. These happenings picture a coming rapture of the Church followed by the immediate outpouring of God's wrath found in the seven bowl judgments.

- The valley of Hinnom pictures eternal judgment in Hell, while Sheol was the abode of the righteous dead in "paradise" until Christ liberated souls in paradise to Heaven—the Scriptures mention a "first heaven" or atmosphere around our world, a "third heaven" or place where God dwells, and by implication, the "second heaven" would be our cosmos.

- Following the literal millennium period, unbelievers will be judged to eternal punishment away from God and God's people. This judgment, called the second death, precludes the notion that a Christian may forfeit their salvation after first trusting in Christ, "dying" again.

Chapter 20

A New Heaven—A New Earth

Then I saw a new heaven and a new earth, for the first heaven and the first earth had passed away and there was no longer any sea.

—Revelation 21:1

But do not forget this one thing . . . with the LORD a day is like a thousand years, and a thousand years are like a day. The LORD is not slow keeping His promise, as some understand slowness. He is patient with you, not wanting anyone to perish, but everyone to come to repentance . . . the day of the **Lord** will come like a thief. The heavens will disappear with a roar; the elements will be destroyed by fire, and the earth and everything in it will be laid bare. Since everything will be destroyed in this way, what kind of people ought you to be . . . live holy and godly lives as you look forward to the day of God and speed its coming. That day will bring about the destruction of the heavens by fire, and the elements will melt in the heat . . . in keeping with His promise we are looking forward to a new heaven and a new earth, the home of righteousness.

—2 Peter 3:8–10

Peter counseled the Church to live holy lives since this cursed world and all it has to offer in the present will be destroyed.

A dreadful day of the LORD is coming (Joel 2:11). That day will bring about the destruction of the cosmos in a fiery cataclysm. Peter states that the heavens will disappear with a roar—undoubtedly a tremendous noise! Peter and John declare there will be a new heaven to replace the former heavens!

In the previous chapter, we discussed the third heaven as the paradise or dwelling place of God. The skies, or visible heavens, comprise the first heaven. Between the first and third heavens lies the vast void of outer space, or the second heaven. The unfathomable dimensions of the universe can very well be a chasm impossible to pass between Hell, located in the depths of the earth, and the heavenly abode of God and the holy angels.

Before the time of Noah, the earth had never experienced rain. The earth was instead watered from below ground streams (Genesis 2:5–6). After sin entered the world, man became increasingly corrupt, violent, and evil (Genesis 6:5–12). Sinners of the ancient world were judged and died by the flood. Although the world will never experience again a complete deluge, the "first heaven" of our atmosphere is a constant source of driving rain, fierce winds, and lightning. Skies now blackened by clouds filled with potential for hail, snow, and rain will disappear, to be replaced with the new heaven that is coming. Following the millennium, death and Hades will be taken from the lowest depths of the earth and will be cast into the lake of burning sulfur. The great chasm of outer space will dissolve and the dwelling place of God will descend to rest upon the glorious new earth.

What was the "sea" seen by Daniel and John? John foresaw a new heaven and new earth, and he records that there will be "no more sea." Daniel had a vision with four great beasts "arising from the sea" (Daniel 7:2–3). The beasts represent four gentile empires emerging from the sea of humanity. The sea represents unsaved humankind—Jesus told Simon Peter he would become a "fisher of men." Jesus compared Heaven's kingdom to a fisherman's net catching diverse fish (Matthew 13:47). Besides no more "sea of men" to fish from (all are judged to heaven or hell), perhaps the literal oceans also cease to exist after the millennium as the new earth parallels the creation before our earth lay under a curse.

Before the Noahic flood, the earth's water derived from underground springs. We may deduce that our then-rich atmosphere contained water vapor misting the lush vegetation. There were no rainstorms at that time. Storm-tossed seas were one of the results of the earth's curse—there no longer will be any sea following the millennium. The sea is also a symbol of unsaved humanity in which disciples can fish for men. During the outpouring of God's wrath on the earth, the second angel will pour out God's bowl on the sea and living things in the sea will die (Revelation 16:3). After the millennium, the wicked are cast into the lake of fire and God makes His dwelling place with the righteous. With a new heaven and a new earth, there is no longer a need for any sea in which to "fish for men."

From the day Jesus ascended into Heaven, Christians have awaited the fulfillment of the Lord's promised return to Earth. Peter addressed the incorrect perception that the Lord is tardy in fulfilling His promise to return to establish His literal earthly kingdom. The Lord is not slow to act but quite merciful in His dealings with men. He patiently allows time to pass—unbelievers receive many opportunities to become Christians. One thousand years seems like a great deal of time to mortal man who expects seventy, perhaps eighty years, in his span. God is the Father of eternity in contrast: patient and beyond the influence of time and space.

"A day is like one thousand years, and one thousand years is like a day with God" (2Peter 3: 8). This language is recognized as metaphor, but I believe there are numerous literal applications to the concept of a thousand years as a day in God's calendar plan.

The day of the LORD, for example, is more than a single twenty-four-hour period of time. It is an extended time when God's enemies are overthrown (see Isaiah 2:12–21; 13:9–16; Joel 1:15–2:11; Zechariah 14:1–5), followed by an earthly reign of Christ (Zechariah 14:16–21; 2 Peter 6–12; Revelation 20:4–6), and is completed following the millennium when the wicked are judged and the earth is renewed by fire (Zephaniah 1:1–3, 14–18; 2 Peter 3:12; Revelation 20:7–9; 21:1).

The day of the LORD spans great events just before, and immediately following, the one thousand-year millennium period. If, with the Lord a day is like a thousand years, it must be noted that *the day* of the LORD is the "day" the Church is raptured and wrath is poured upon the earth (Revelation 15:1) *tacked onto* the entire thousand-year period spanning the resurrection of the righteous for reward (Matthew 24:31; Mark 13:27; Revelation 14:15–16; 20:4) *and* the time of the white throne judgment of unbelievers for punishment (Revelation 20:5–11–15).

> "Multitudes who sleep in the dust of the earth will awake: some to everlasting life, others to shame and everlasting contempt."
> Daniel 12:2

Daniel wrote of a time of great distress, commonly known as the "tribulation." According to the account in Revelation 20, martyrs of Antichrist's reign will resurrect and reign with Christ a thousand years. Others are not raised to life before the millennium ends. Daniel foresaw a time when the deceased arise to eternal life or to damnation. Although there are one thousand years between the first resurrection and the resurrection of those who stand for judgment (see Revelation 20:5–6, 11–12), both events occur during the day of the LORD.

"For my Father's will is that everyone who looks the Son and believes in him shall have eternal life, and I will raise him up at the last day." John 6:40

The righteous rise to life at the last day of this present evil age. The last day occurs in strength when the seventh angel sounds His trumpet (Revelation 11:15–17) and the seven bowls filled with God's wrath begin to pour onto the earth. This last day of the rule of Satan over our fallen world marks the beginning of the thousand-year period known as the day of the LORD.

This present evil age has lasted approximately 6,000 years and will be someday followed by a thousand-year righteous reign of Christ on Earth. "With the Lord a day is like a thousand years." The six days of creation were followed by a Sabbath day of rest. This pattern of days may foreshadow the 6,000 years of this wicked world followed by one thousand years comprising the great day of the LORD. Man has endured 6,000 years of painful toil, laboring so he could he could eat from the cursed ground (Genesis 3:17–19). The millennium in contrast signals a time of renewal for the earth and peace for man. Men shall rest from making war (Isaiah 2:4). At the end of the millennium, the last rebellion of man is quashed—as the dead rise for final judgment.

For our struggle is not against flesh and blood, but against the rulers, against the authorities, against the powers of this dark world and against the spiritual forces of evil in the heavenly realms. Ephesians 6:12

This dark, sin-corrupt world and the heavenly realms visited now by spiritual evil forces will be consumed in an inferno. The new Heaven and Earth will be free from all impurity. The eternal kingdom cannot be defiled by anyone who does what is shameful or deceitful (Revelation 21:27). The dwelling of God will be with men—men purchased by the blood of Christ (Revelation 5:9; 21:3).

> For our light and momentary troubles are achieving for us an eternal glory that far outweighs them all. So we fix our eyes not on what is seen, but what is unseen. For what is seen is temporary, but what is unseen is eternal. 2 Corinthians 4:17–18

> "He will wipe every tear from their eyes. There will be no more death or mourning or crying or pain, for the old order of things has passed away." Revelation 21:4

Today, numerous media outlets report the news. We read newspapers and magazines or witness riots, fires, and war's carnage live on the radio, on television, or by accessing the Internet. Most media reports are tragic in nature, sensationalized by placing the most graphic images at the top of each report. Acts of violence, marital infidelities, and political corruption are fodder for a hungry media mill, grinding out stories around the clock. The impact of this barrage of gloomy news is emotionally devastating—many have become chronically depressed. Others seek to find escape from what they view as hopeless by turning to alcohol or other drugs. A few seek tragic notoriety by committing copycat crimes.

It is an old scheme of the devil to overwhelm the Christian believers with the troubles of this world. When a Christian focuses on his inadequacy and not Christ's sufficiency, he becomes ineffective in witness and prayer. Compared to the weight of eternal glory, our problems and trials are momentary and light. We are exhorted to encourage others with words of hope, focusing on the faithfulness of God to fulfill all His promises (see John 14:1–4; 1 Thessalonians 5:18).

Since the 1960s, steep rises in crime and sharp declines in morality have impacted Western culture and the world. The baby boomer generation was birthed following World War II when Israel was again declared a sovereign Jewish nation. This same generation, which benefited greatly from postwar prosperity, utterly rejected traditional values. During the same decade in which Israel came into control of a unified Jerusalem, the cry of "Sex, Drugs, and Rock n' Roll!" rang from America's college campuses and in Europe.

I believe this generation, the generation legalizing abortion, seeking to sanction same sex marriages, promoting so-called "safe sex," and scourging references to God and the Bible in public life is the generation that shall witness the Second Coming of Jesus Christ.

> "Now learn this lesson from the fig tree: As soon as its twigs get tender and its leaves come out, you know that summer is near. Even so, when you see all these things, you know that it is near, right at the door. I tell you the truth, this generation will certainly not pass away until all these things have happened." Matthew 24:32–34

Numerous Bible references concern the gathering of the outcasts of Israel. Not only is it miraculous that many of the Jewish people have returned to the Promised Land, but also the Hebrew language, in dim use since the Babylonian captivity twenty-five hundred years ago, is revived.

How is modern Israel a witness of the Second Coming of Christ?

> "Who has ever heard of such a thing? Who has ever seen such things? Can a country be born in a day or a nation be brought forth in a moment?" Isaiah 66:8a

After centuries of foreign domination and Diaspora, the United Nations birthed Israel in a single day in the same way that God birthed a nation in a day from Egyptian bondage. The fig tree is symbolic of Israel (Hosea 9:10; Luke 13:6–9). Jesus foretold of a future generation that would be alive to see the predicted signs that would occur *just before* His return. "This generation will certainly not pass away" refers to the generation that would be alive to witness the fig tree sprout its leaves. Israel, the fig tree, was declared a nation in 1948—though the nation did not control the holy city of Jerusalem until 1967.

The children of Israel during the time of Moses were disobedient and refused to go up and possess the Promised Land. As a punishment, they wandered for forty years in the desert until that wicked generation died in the desert (Numbers 14:27–32). If we consider forty years a biblical generation, perhaps some of the baby boomers witnessing the capture of historic Jerusalem in '67 may live to see the return of Christ.

Today, we are witnessing the attempt to divide Jerusalem and remove the control of the city from Jewish hands. The results of the Middle East "peace process" have been anything but peaceful! The day of the LORD will come at a time when people are proclaiming peace and safety and destruction will suddenly come upon them (1 Thessalonians 5:3). The day of the LORD is a day when all the nations of the world gather to fight against Jerusalem (Zechariah 14:2).

We are living in a generation that is perhaps as violent as the days of Noah and as promiscuous as the days of Sodom and Gomorrah. We must never grow weary or lose heart; we must focus upon eternal things, stand in faith. Christians have the mind of Christ Jesus who endured the cross scorning its shame because He was able to look past the suffering to see the joy our salvation would bring (Hebrews 12:2). We must endure persecution for a short while, but we will enjoy heavenly reward for eternity:

"Even so, when you see all these things, you know that it is near, right at the door." Matthew 24:33

"Behold, I am coming soon! My reward is with me, and I will give to everyone according to what he has done. I am the Alpha and the Omega, the First and the Last, the Beginning and the End." Revelation 22:12–13

He who testifies to these things says, "Yes, I am coming soon." Amen. Come, Lord Jesus. The grace of the Lord Jesus be with God's people. Amen. Revelation 22:20–21

Summary of Chapter Twenty

- A new Heaven and Earth are promised following the millennium (Revelation 21:1).
- We have powerful pictures in Revelation of a better tomorrow:

    o no more sea (no "sea" of wicked humanity from which Christians "fish" for believers)

    o the day of the LORD (a thousand-year time span of righteousness between the bowl judgments and final battle and judgment)

    o an eternal abode with God where there will be no mourning, pain, or death

- Jesus gave numerous indications of when His return was near, "right at the door." An honest examination of current events must allow for the possibility of the tribulation and Christ's glorious return to occur during our lifetime (Matthew 24:33).

Post Script

One Final Argument

The First Resurrection

Listen, I tell you a mystery: We will not all sleep, but we will all be changed—in a flash, in the twinkling of an eye, at the last trumpet. For the trumpet will sound, the dead will be raised imperishable, and we will be changed.

—1 Corinthians 15:51–52

For the Lord himself will come down from heaven, with a loud command, with the voice of the archangel and with the trumpet call of God, and the dead in Christ will rise first. After that, we who are still alive and are left will be caught up together with them in the clouds to meet the Lord in the air. And so we will be with the Lord forever.

—1 Thessalonians 4:16–17

Rapture comes from the phrase "caught up" in 1 Thessalonians 4:17. In the Greek, the word is *harpazo*: "to seize upon by force," "to snatch up." The Latin translators used the word *rapturo*.

When will those who are alive be raptured (caught up) to meet the Lord in the air? It is clearly stated in 1 Thessalonians 4:16–17 that the rapture or snatching away of those who are alive when Christ returns will occur after the dead are resurrected to eternal life.

When will the dead be raised—before or after the reign of the Antichrist?

> I saw thrones on which were seated those who had been given authority to judge. And I saw the souls of those who had been beheaded because of their testimony for Jesus and because of the word of God. They had not worshiped the beast or his image and had not received his mark on their foreheads or their hands. They came to life and reigned with Christ a thousand years. (The rest of the dead did not come to life until the thousand years were ended.) This is the first resurrection. Revelation 20: 4–5

Those who had not worshiped the beast or his image were slain for their testimony. These righteous dead are blessed to be among those who will take part in the first resurrection. It is evident from the above passage that the first resurrection will take place after the reign of the Antichrist. Since the rapture does not take place until the resurrection of the righteous, these passages comprise another proof text that there will not be a pre-tribulation rapture.

For those who claim that there are many resurrections, please note that there is a difference between being raised from the dead and resurrection to a "glorified body." In both the Old and New Testament there are several accounts of those raised from the dead by prophets, apostles and Adonai Yeshua (the Lord Jesus). Yet, none were raised immortal in glorified bodies. At the first resurrection (Revelation 20:5), all the righteous are raised to life. After the Millennium, will come the "great white throne judgment" (Revelation 20:11), and all those not found in the "book of life" are cast into the lake of fire (Revelation 20:14–15).

Do you know for sure that your name is written in the book of life?

Even so, come, Lord Jesus.

About the Author

Steven L. Sherman is founder and president of "Just Pray NO!" Ltd. This non-profit organization is a prayer and intercession ministry that has traveled to 118 countries and in twenty-three languages. Today, the "Just Pray NO!" Annual Worldwide Weekend of Prayer and Unity has prayer partners and supporting churches ministering to the victims of drug and alcohol abuse in all 50 states and on six continents. If you need help with an addiction problem or want to participate in the annual prayer event, then visit the ministry's web site by logging on to http://justprayno.org.

Mr. Sherman was born in New York City, where he has made frequent appearances on Christian radio and television to help promote his work. He is an educator licensed by New York State and in Florida to teach Health and Physical Education and is a certified Family Living Instructor. Steven Sherman is a gifted Bible Studies teacher who shares Scripture in light of his Jewish heritage. If you are interested in learning the Bible in its historical context of Jewish culture, then you are welcome to visit his teaching web site at http://lastdayscalendar.net.

Mr. Sherman has five children and two grandchildren, Alexandria, age five, and Benjamin, who was born October 19, 1997, on his 50th birthday. The Shermans currently reside in Dunedin, Florida.

Printed in the United States
147547LV00005B/12/A